D0557899

The
Lost Roads
Project

A Walk-in Book of Arkansas

The Lost Roads Project

A Walk-in Book of Arkansas

by C. D. Wright

photographs by Deborah Luster

THE UNIVERSITY OF ARKANSAS PRESS
Fayetteville 1994

Manufactured in Korea

98 97 96 95 94   5 4 3 2 1

Designed by Liz Lester

The paper used in this publication meets the minimum requirements
of the American National Standard for Permanence of Paper for
Printed Library Materials Z39.48-1984. ∞

Library of Congress Cataloging-in-Publication Data

Wright, C. D., 1949–
    The lost roads project: a walk-in book of Arkansas / by C. D.
Wright; photographs by Deborah Luster.
        p. cm.
    Includes bibliographical references.
    ISBN 1–55728–362–1 (paper)
    1. Authors, American—Arkansas—Biography. 2. Arkansas—
Literary collections. 3. American literature—Arkansas. I. Luster,
Deborah. II. Title.
PS266.A8W75 1994
810.9'9767—dc20   94–30424
                                                       CIP

*The author wishes to express deepest thanks to the Lila Wallace-Reader's
Digest Fund for the Writer's Award which made this initiative possible.*

for my mother, Alyce E. Wright,
and my father, Ernie Edward Wright,
for Brecht Wright Gander, my son

When you take the lost road
You find the bright feathers of morning
Laid out in proportion to snow and light
And when the snow gets lost on the road
Then the hot wind might blow from the south
And there is sadness in bed for twenty centuries
And everyone is chewing the grass on the graves again.

—from "Circle of Lorca" by Frank Stanford

Come, it is time to be born.

—from "Pane of Vision" by Henry Dumas

big with tenderness

—from "Tell Our Daughters" by Besmilr Brigham

Acknowledgments

Shirley Abbott: from *Womenfolks*. Copyright © 1983 by Shirley Abbott, published by Ticknor and Fields. Reprinted by permission of the press.

Maya Angelou: from *I Know Why the Caged Bird Sings*. Copyright © 1969 by Maya Angelou. Reprinted by permission of Random House, Inc.

Margaret Jones Bolsterli: from *Born in the Delta: Reflections on the Making of a Southern White Sensibility*. Copyright © 1991 by Margaret Jones Bolsterli, published by University of Tennessee Press. Reprinted by permission of the press.

Besmilr Brigham: "Heaved from the Earth" from *Heaved from the Earth*. Copyright © 1969, 1970, 1971 by Besmilr Brigham. Reprinted by permission of Alfred A. Knopf, Inc.

Dee Brown: from *Bury My Heart at Wounded Knee: An Indian History of the American West*. Copyright © 1970 by Dee Brown. Reprinted by permission of Henry Holt and Company, Inc.

Andrea Hollander Budy: "Pigs" from *House without a Dreamer*. Copyright © 1993 by Andrea Hollander Budy. Reprinted by permission of Story Line Press.

Jack Butler: from *Living in Little Rock with Miss Little Rock*. Copyright © 1993 by Jack Butler. Reprinted by permission of Alfred A. Knopf, Inc.

Crescent Dragonwagon: "Skillet-Sizzled Buttermilk Cornbread" from *Dairy Hollow House Soup and Bread: A Country Inn Cookbook*. Copyright © 1992 by Crescent Dragonwagon. Reprinted by permission of Workman Publishing Company, Inc. All rights reserved.

Henry Dumas: from "Goodbye, Sweetwater," from *Goodbye, Sweetwater: New and Selected Stories of Henry Dumas,* edited by Eugene B. Redmond. Copyright © 1988 by Loretta Dumas and Eugene B. Redmond, published by Thunder's Mouth Press. Reprinted by permission of the press.

Donald Harington: from *Some Other Place. The Right Place.* Copyright © 1972 by Donald Harington. Reprinted by permission of Harcourt Brace & Company.

Key Assistance

Peter Armitage: designer

Robert Cochran: director, Center for Arkansas and Regional Studies, state sponsor, consultant

Walter Feldman: broadside designer, printer, woodcut artist

Forrest Gander: videographer

Richard Johnson: composer and guitarist; with Jud Martindale, percussionist

Lila Wallace-Reader's Digest Fund: with special guidance from Marcie Hinand and additional counsel from Sheila Murphy

Deborah Luster: photographer

Michael Luster: folklorist, consultant, interviewer

John Romano: Portfolio Box, Inc.

Douglas Stowe: craftsman

Kathy P. Thompson: artist

Samuel Truitt: research assistant, Brown University

Miller Williams: director, University of Arkansas Press

Gratitude is also due Barbara Bloemink, curator; Henri Linton, chair, Art Department, University of Arkansas at Pine Bluff; Michael Dabrishus, director, and Andrea Campbell, assistant director, Special Collections, Mullins Library, University of Arkansas; Michelle Mankins, student research assistant; Stephen Larson, Dictation Equipment Center, Inc.; Debbie Neel, postmaster of Horatio; Susan Saidenburg, exhibitions director, New York Public Library; John Cole, director, Center for the Book, Library of Congress; Margaret Brown, video-editor; Frank Rothman, provost, Brown University; Bryan Shepp, dean of the faculty, Brown University; Diana Johnson, director, Winston-Bell Gallery, Brown University; Rita H. Warnock, curator of broadsides, Harris Collection, John Hay Library, University of Arkansas; Bubba Sullivan, proprietor, Blues Corner Records, Helena; David Westmoreland, English curriculum specialist, Arkansas Department of Education; Beverly Lindsey, director, Department of Arkansas Heritage; Sally Williams, coordinator, Arkansas Arts Council; Ronnie Nichols, executive director, Old State House; Bill Gatewood, director of exhibitions, Old State House; Rick Hadley, design director, Dewitt-Wallace

Museum; Mary Gay Shipley, proprietor, The Book Rack, Blytheville; Ernie E. Wright, fact finder; Don Lee, desktop publishing services; John Coghlan and Debbie Bowen, University of Arkansas Press; Edmund White, writer; Susan Burden, chair, Deer High School Humanities Department; the community and schools of Deer; Brandy Rocole, Betsy Morphis, and Angel Elam; inmates and staff of the North Central Unit, Arkansas Department of Corrections, Calico Rock; Rex and Mary Giles; Nick Ames; Misty and Ashley Giles; Kelly Hancock; John Mitchell; Helen Copeland Gamble; Jimmy and Cleatha Driftwood; Adella Hale; Bill Willett; Mr. and Mrs. Hopkins of Poyen; Hulian V. Webb; Robert Walker; Johnny Neville; Mike Hall; Tamondo Stafford; Jerry Weaver aka Damian the Magician; Darrell Thomas; Doris and Sam Carr; Eddie Walton and Frank Frost; Houston Stackhouse Jr.; Robert Titus; Roy Brigham; Mr. and Mrs. Priest of De Valls Bluff; C. L. Patton; Duane; Anita Huffington and Hank Sutter; Peter Tooker; Brecht Gander; photographers, Carolyn DeMeritt, Cathy Crowell, Tom Rankin, John A. Langston, Denny Moers.

Contents

Writers

Biographies

Photographs

Introduction

Due to Arkansas's relative isolation from a coast or major metropolis, its dramatically distinct topographies, both mountain and delta, and its cornucopia of natural resources vaunting everything from rice to diamonds, the lore holds that a fence, invisible to strangers, separates Arkansas from the rest of the nation. The state's artists among other bodacious types have routinely ignored this fabled border. Nevertheless, there is a persistent identification—as striking as a blazed tree—which marks the lexicon of its writers, the apertures of its photographers, the tunings of its musicians, the very materials employed by its sculptors. The sum of the arts convene to aestheticize, mythologize, and historicize the Wonder State's cultural independence. My aim is to present not a unified vision, but an original, kindred one which gives particular expression to a particular place. The focus here is literary, though other genres and other media will elaborate the literature I have elected to feature.

My stance is that Arkansas culture, the artful expression of an internally autonomous territory in letters, has been both precisely and uncommonly expressed, and that this record is a cause for assertion. The Lost Roads Project may be a panegyric to our common tome; magnolia-mongering it is not. I arkansas. Others I have known, or have had the honor to meet in print, arkansas also. It is neither a hieratic nor a hermetic tongue, but it is almost distinct. The inexorable course of cultural assimilation and the willful course of historical amnesia put the distinction at risk. Because I consider assimilation and amnesia artistic violations, I will try to emblazon the differences expressed here on the bark of the trees yet standing.

The survey that follows is not designed to be definitive. This is my primer, my Arkansas reader. My own reading has been neither systematic nor exhaustive. It has been deliberately limited. I knew to take the main roads, however familiar, but I was also inclined to be led along the state's literary traces, its submerged missions, vacated county seats, unkept graves, and broken levees. I wanted to make a few recoveries and a few discoveries, for my own satisfaction. It is my conviction that culture is our primary product; its expression is a necessity. Creative human work and thought is produced, regularly, and when permissible, on a daily basis, out of necessity, by people with more than and less than adequate means. It is my conviction that the subset of our culture known as literature is not the private preserve of the formally educated, but an ever-expanding, ever-changing mindscape. The vitality of a literature depends upon its capacity for inclusion and change. The literature of a given state is obviously an arbitrary boundary. Any literature's vitality is both dependent upon its capacity to take root, to grow, and its urge to overreach arbitrary boundaries. Poet Margaret Avison holds that literature results when every word is written in the full light of all a writer knows. I borrow her statement as an ambitious definition.

What follows is a selection; it is built upon previous selections modified by what I think I know. The historical material is extremely compressed as these chronologies are abundantly, amply treated in other sources. As the time drew more proximate, I lingered longer over individual authors, leaving more and more authors by the wayside—for the next journey and the next. Where a spur appeared, it was often taken, and what I found at the end of that spur might very well have been chosen to replace something back on the main line. I encourage others, ired or inspired by the line I have chosen, to create an opposing or apposing one.

Prior to the mid-sixteenth century, the *terra incognita* named for its original people the Quapaws, or Arkansea, had been trespassed in the vicinity of Sunflower Landing (twenty miles south of Helena). The region, that is to say, had been irrevocably penetrated by white men, horses, hogs et al., and dutifully described by the literati of Hernando de Soto's party, the first publication from which *The True Relation of the Gentleman of Elvas* appeared in Portugal in 1557, fifteen years after the fact; fifteen years after the blood-drenched, malarial conquistador De Soto died in Louisiana, aged forty-two. The Portuguese soldier's account is more than two hundred pages long and details, in unassuming prose, the discovery, the hardship, the sport, and the cruelties of the De Soto itinerary. The other expedition chronicles are three: a brief official report to the King of Spain, the diary of De Soto's private secretary, and a secondhand, chivalric account by the colonized Peruvian scholar known as The Inca.

A hundred years passed. French expeditions succeeded the Spanish. The Jesuit priest Marquette came down from Quebec with the fur trader and geographer Joliet to the mouth of the Arkansas in search of the Vermilion Sea. They were followed by the ill-fated Sieur de La Salle and his Sicilian second, Henri de Tonti, who would establish, after a fashion, Arkansas Post. Bernard de la Harpe journeyed up the Mississippi from New Orleans in 1722, then upriver on the Arkansas to the stone outcrop he called the "Little Rock." More reports entered the documentary record.

Back at the mouth of the river, the Post clung to its existence, flying, back and forth, French and Spanish colors until the Louisiana Purchase. Arkansas Post became the territorial capital in 1819 but acquiesced to Little Rock in 1821, and in 1855 it lost its diminutive county-seat status when the seat repaired to De Witt. Arkansas Post was not situated to be a center of government. There was never any question of it becoming a literary powder keg. Remained, the bois d'arc trees.[1]

The rightful claimants to the entire, the Quapaws, the paradisiacal Down Stream People, were swiftly reduced by the European bequeathal of smallpox—then further reduced by firearms, by debt, by booze, along with demeaning, soon-to-be-defied treaties, then gone. They may have been thousands as some reported, or only four villages. Then they were none. The missionaries continued to traipse through, penning their experiences and observations. However, the next documents of any literary bent, and the first in English, would not enter the territorial frame until the nineteenth century. Explorations of the Ouachita Valley to the hot springs were commissioned by Thomas Jefferson and reported by William Dunbar and Dr. George Hunter, but it would be left to the English-born botanist Thomas Nuttall to exact a description of the vaporous locale, Hot Springs.

Those intrepid scientists came a-naming: Thomas Nuttall (1786–1859), New York-born geologist Henry Rowe Schoolcraft (1793–1864) whose survey of lead mines extended to descriptions of river trade and folk life of the Indians and frontier inhabitants, and English geologist George W. Featherstonhaugh (1780–1866). They described, cited, specified; they fixed. Each of these gentlemen had a turn at exploring Hot Springs. None offered geological explanations for the springs' presence. The town was thirty years from incorporation when Nuttall and Schoolcraft passed through in the traces of the Dunbar and Hunter duo sent by President Jefferson. It was already a primitive spa. Says Schoolcraft:

"A vein of singular earth, a kind of *lithomarge,* is also found at the springs. It is soft, like clay, of a soponaceous feel, and of a texture so delicately fine, that it feels to the touch like satin. It would probably operate as a detergent to the oil particles of newly woven cloth, and in this respect answer the purpose of *fuller's earth.*"[2] Nuttall observed that "The water charged with an excess of carbonic acid, holding lime in solution, deposits a calcareous tufa, which incrusts leaves, moss, or any other substance which it meets in its course, to the great surprise of the ignorant, who commonly pronounce them petrefactions."[3] Featherstonhaugh, however, had this to say: "How invalids contrive to be comfortable, who come to this ragged place, I cannot imagine, yet I understand that ten or a dozen people are often crammed into this room, which my son and myself found much too small for two . . . All roads of every kind terminate at the Hot Springs; beyond them there is nothing but the unbroken wilderness . . ."[4] Featherstonhaugh, it seems, missed his high tea.

A quarter of the way into the 1800s, one of the century's most unmediated lives, Sequoyah, the Cherokee whose English name was George Guess and who came to be referred to as the American Cadmus, achieved a tool of learning unrivaled by a single intelligence in the history of letters—an alphabet, more properly, a syllabary of eighty-six characters for the Cherokee language. Without ever attending school or learning the white man's language; with bark and berry juice, stones and dirt; with the singular resources of his own imagination, he invented corresponding characters for the sense and sound, construction and inflection of his people's speech. By 1828 the type for the syllabary was cast. In February the first issue of the *Cherokee Phoenix* appeared. Literacy raged across the Cherokee Nation, a claim no contemporary people in the United States could make. One observer traveling through the territory in 1828—weeks prior to the initial printing of the *Phoenix* paper—wrote: "I frequently saw as I rode from place to place, Cherokee letters painted or cut on the trees by the roadside, on fences, houses, and often on pieces of bark or board, lying about the houses . . . Bark, trees, fences, the walls of houses, &c., answered the purpose of slates . . . That the mass of a people, without schools or books, should by mutual assistance, without extraneous impulse or aid, acquire the art of reading, and that in a character wholly original, is, I believe, a phenomenon unexampled in modern times."[5] Nonetheless, Sequoyah's wife and his tribesmen thought the silent, limping blacksmith was a bum, off his nut to boot, which is why he ended up running a refinery—boiling salt down in big black pots—outside of Dwight Mission (now under Greer's Ferry Lake). Alone, in Arkansas, he completed his solemn, visionary project. After the Removal, the septua- or octogenarian, as the date of his birth is disputed, and a few disciples commenced a search for a lost band of Cherokees in Mexico. Sequoyah sought to account for every stray Cherokee soul. He is reported to have found these extended members of the nation and to have been writing an account of his journey, though he did not survive to return. In 1852 his widow, Sally Guess, was directed to receive a three-hundred-dollar annual pension which had been set aside by the Cherokee council for Sequoyah. Grant Foreman's early biographical sketch remarks: "This was probably the first literary pension in American history, and certainly the first and only one ever granted by an Indian tribe."[6]

One of the founders of Dwight Mission (1820) where Sequoyah settled was the zealous Reverend Cephas Washburn. In 1864 he published his *Reminiscences of the Indians*. His son, painter Edward Payson Washburn, illustrated the central archetype of Arkansas folk literature with his two captioned paintings of *The Arkansas Traveler*. The missionary and his son are buried in Mount Holly Cemetery in Little Rock, along with other notable scribblers of the state, including poet John Gould Fletcher.

Before the Civil War, fiction was being written about Arkansas mostly by men from elsewhere. Frederick Gerstacker (1816–1872) authored seventy books and over four hundred stories and travel sketches (altogether too many), among them two novels and numerous stories fabricated from his travels in the state between 1838 and 1841. Corrupted at a very early age by *Robinson Crusoe* and James Fenimore Cooper, the twenty-one-year-old son of German opera singers crossed into Arkansas on the Current River in January of 1838, free at last of bourgeois constraints and expectations. Thirty years later, he voyaged from Germany to the backwoods again, only to find his old friends dead and his old grass hills overgrown in the wake of the Civil War. In truth, Gerstacker only accidentally "made a writer" when his mother began publishing his diaries in advance of his first return to Germany. Thereafter, he became a speedwriter, in part from economic necessity; in part from an incapacity to adapt to a sedentary job. Gerstacker was more socially motivated than the scientists who preceded him in the frontier. He held, in a sense, to a higher code, that the guest should honor his host even if what the host had to offer was a strip of greasy meat and a filthy floor. While his fiction is at its best in its nonfictive components, he was perfectly qualified to entertain while he fed valuable information through the works. An excellent collection of Gerstacker's tales and sketches has been published recently: *In the Arkansas Backwoods,* edited and translated by James William Miller (University of Missouri Press, 1991). I relied on it for what seems a more enlivening, even-handed evaluation of the writer than Gerstacker is usually dealt.

Bostonian Albert Pike made Van Buren his home, then later moved to Little Rock. Pike fell squarely into the *manqué* category as a poet, and some would say as a soldier. As a lawyer, newspaper editor, and husband, perhaps he attained his expected level. On a 1988 literary map of the American South, General Pike is Arkansas's only listing. This perverse fact alone is cause for further investigation. Mark Twain disembarked in Helena and makes references to certain island numbers claimed by the state, but between the Hannibals of Missouri and the Hartfords of Connecticut, Twain is properly charted. On similarly flimsy grounds twentieth-century writers Ernest Hemingway, Lewis Nordan, and Ellen Douglas have been cast as Arkansas writers, even though their writings do not take root in the state. A case could be made for some of the short fiction of Richard Wright, whose childhood stays in Elaine and West Helena passed the high-water mark, and for passages of Ellen Gilchrist, whose character composites can be glimpsed circling a certain town square.

Charles Fenton Mercer Noland is the often-cited, infrequently quoted backwoods humorist whose chief contribution may be the letters he printed in the *Spirit of the Times,* a weekly New York sporting magazine, in the persona of backwoodsman Pete Whetstone. An entire fictitious family attends Whetstone, along with a host of neighbors and animals: his hounds Sharptooth, General Jackson, and June; his horses Bussing Coon and Dry Bones; and his donkey Levi. He created the midsouth position Garrison Keillor currently occupies for the midwest. Though a Virginian by birth, Noland came to Arkansas in 1826 after being dismissed from West Point when he was eighteen. His father had been appointed to direct the U.S. Land Office in Batesville. Soon enough, Noland's provocative letters obliged him to duel Gov. John Pope's nephew, who died from the wounds inflicted by Noland. He was nevertheless a star in Arkansas political life. He took Arkansas's first constitution to Washington.[7] He edited the *Batesville Eagle,* then the *Arkansas Gazette.* Despite the tuberculosis to which Colonel Noland succumbed at fifty, he was one of the state's most celebrated, energetic scribes, colorfully profiled in Alfred W. Arrington's *The Lives and Adventures of the Desperadoes of the South-West* (1848):

"Sunday, he will write an eloquent dissertation on religion; Monday, he raw-hides a rogue; Tuesday, he composes a sonnet, set in silver stars, and breathing perfume of roses to some fair maid's eyebrows; Wednesday, he fights a duel, and sends a bit of lead whizzing through the head or heart of some luckless desper-adoe; Thursday, he does up brown the personal character and political conduct of senators Sevier and Ashley; Friday, he goes to the ball, dressed in the most finical superfluity of the fashion, and shines the soul of wit, and the sun of merry badinage, among all the gay gentlemen, and the king supreme of all tender hearts among the ladies. And, to close the triumphs of the week, on Saturday night, he is off thirty miles to a country dance, in the Ozark Mountains, where they 'trip it on the light fantastic toe,' in the famous jig of 'double shuffle,' around a roaring log-heap fire in the woods, all night long . . . while between each dance Fent Noland sings some beautiful wild song, such as 'Lucy Neal,' or 'Julianna Johnson,' or that melody most serene, 'Such a Gitten Up Stairs!' "[8] Arrington was a man of some versatility himself, being an itinerant Methodist preacher, a lawyer, legislator, judge, and yet another poet *manqué*.

Pete Whetstone's often-quoted contemporary was the humorist T. B. Thorpe, whose "Big Bear of Arkansas" is as big as you would imagine a cre-ation b'ar to be. Thorpe was a northerner who settled temporarily in Louisiana, but he is best remembered for this backwoods whopper told to city men by the narrator from his steamboat berth en route to Arkansas. The tale snakes slowly through the animal kingdom, wherein the teller begins by felling a wild turkey of no less than forty pounds, and once shot, "he bust open behind, and the way the pound gobs of tallow rolled out of the opening was perfectly beautiful."[9] This took place in the only possible place, "the creation state, the finishing-up country; a state where the *sile* runs down to the centre of the 'arth and gov-ernment gives you a title to every inch of it. Then its airs—just breathe them, and they will make you snort like a horse."[10]

The first Arkansas author to fall out of favor with his subject was Opie Read. He was born in 1852 in Tennessee. A printer by training, Read edited *The Prairie Flower* in Carlisle, another paper in Conway, and the *Arkansas Gazette* in Little Rock. He also founded a witty weekly, *The Arkansas Traveler,* which he moved to Chicago in the 1880s. This was a period when there were three hundred newspapers in Arkansas, and we are not talking the Gannett gang. There actu-ally were as many different owners with whom to differ. Some of the editors moved from one paper to another. Opie Read was among these tramp journalists. His humor was adroit, delivered from the inside, and not always appreciated. Fifty years later it would be Vance Randolph's turn to reap the displeasure of his beloved subject, the hillbilly, among whom he could likewise claim an enduring, not always endearing, membership. According to Randolph, Read spent the best years of his life in Arkansas and penned at least one good hillbilly novel, *Len Gansett* (Chicago, 1888).[11] Both Read and Randolph were capable of deploying what the 1940s' juvenile writer Lois Lenski dubbed full-strength dialect at the expense of its all but recognizable speakers. Both men were burdened more by the limits of realism than by the extravagances of their own imaginations. The local colorists, on the other hand, bore the affliction in reverse.

A number of women were making books before the turn of the century. A couple of them were colorists: Alice French (1850–1934), a Massachusetts native, whose pseudonym was Octave Thanet, came into some plantation land in Clover Bend and wintered on it for thirty years. She drew on Arkansas for several of her books, including *Otto the Knight, and Other Trans-Mississippi Stories* (1891), *We All* (1891), *Expiation* (1901), and *By Inheritance* (1910). She was a writer of strong opinions and considerable descriptive talent. She had more sophisticated story-telling skills but was short the wit and the seasoning of detail of her contemporary Ruth McEnery Stuart (1856–1917), who lived at the state's other extreme, near Hope. While it is repeatedly written that Thanet's dialect was a bit thick, it is no more so than Stuart's, whose minstrel ear has been described as precise. A Chicago reviewer opined, "Mrs. Stuart's Negro dialect comes nearer to perfection than that of any other contemporaneous writer."[12] Shudder. At any rate her stay in Arkansas was confined to the years 1879 to 1883 when she was married to a three-time widower, Alfred Oden Stuart from Washington in Hempstead County. More than seventy-five stories can be credited to Ruth McEnery Stuart. The big river town of Fort Smith was the birthplace of Thyra Samter Winslow, another prolific short-story writer. She began publishing in 1912 after schooling in the East. Her work does not leave a strong impression with me, but she was thriving in the national magazines of the time, as were Thanet and Stuart.

The *Scrapbook of Arkansas Literature* mentions a novel published in 1906 by J. H. Smith (b. 1843) titled *Maudelle: A Novel Founded on Facts Gathered from Living Witnesses*. From the Mosaic Templar's Book, *Racial Possibilities*, I learned that the author is probably the same man as Dr. J. H. Smith, a Little Rock dentist with a bustling biracial practice. The story concerns "illicit commingling" between a senator and his slave with whom he had a child and to whom he willed his estate. Smith writes that the senator was a relative of one of the presidents, that only names and places have been changed, the legitimate names "withheld to avoid embarrassing relatives."[13] The author's preface further states that "strenuous efforts were made to dispossess the child of her property, and it was only after years of litigation that the property was awarded to her by the courts."[14] All of which can probably be verified, and yet the dentist, factual or not, wrote a bona fide novel. The first chapter opens in a blustery snowstorm the night Maudelle is born. The house servant rides "the five thousand dollar stallion" Thunderbolt to fetch the doctor. The scene of Maudelle's birth does not rival, in convincing detail, the birthing in *Anna Karina*. But the tense setting of the home birth, the all-night philosophical conversation between doctor and senator, does equal the Russian's dramatic reach and moral intensity. If the senator of the novel was related to a U.S. President in fact, it was likely a Polk, for elements of this story resurface in Ruth Polk Patterson's exemplary study of her frontier family *The Seed of Sally Good'n* (University Press of Kentucky, 1985).

A Fort Smith girlhood helped—if only through the law of adversity—to shape Katherine Anthony (1877–1965), one of the state's first feminist writers and a fastidiously astute biographer. Her first book, *The Woman Who Must Earn* (1914), signaled her career-long interest in powerful, independent women; biographies of the transcendentalist editor Margaret Fuller, Catherine the Great, Queen Elizabeth, Marie Antoinette, Dollie Madison, and Mercy Otis Warren, "first lady of the revolution," would follow. Her 1925 biography of Catherine the Great was sufficiently definitive to reprint as recently as 1973. Arkansas's prolific Katherine writes of Russia's: "Catherine the Great loved to write. She rose at six o'clock every morning and occupied herself with literary work during the three hours or so which intervened before her Russian servants began to rub their sleepy eyes. She had Spartan methods of awakening herself. First she washed her face and ears with ice; then she drank five cups of the strongest coffee ever brewed. She sat down beside her candle with her pen and wrote in a large free flowing hand, instructions, correspondence, memoirs, fables, histories, comedies. Her output was voluminous. She did not wait to finish one piece before she began another, and the first remained forever unfinished. Everything she wrote is a fragment."[15]

Histories of the state began to log in before 1900. Fay Hempstead's *Pictorial History* was published in 1890; Judge William F. Pope published his personal recollections in 1895. Josiah Shinn's *Pioneers and Makers of Arkansas* came out in 1908. Although it did not appear in print until the 1970s, John Quincy Wolf Sr.'s *Life in the Leatherwoods* (first August House edition, 1988) provides an exceptional view of Calico Rock along the White River in the late nineteenth century. Dallas Herndon's *Centennial History* of the state appeared in 1922, the same year the *Gazette*'s managing editor Fred W. Allsopp published *History of the Arkansas Press for One Hundred Years or More*. Poet/editor Allsopp also wrote a biography of Albert Pike; he compiled an anthology of the poets of the state and cribbed the meter from Longfellow's "Hiawatha" for his interpretation of "The Arkansas Traveler." In James R. Masterson's survey, Allsopp's 1926 version is the eleventh to carve the anecdote of squatter and traveler into the state's identity, if not its collective consciousness.

"The Arkansas Traveler" has been trotted out *ad nauseum* as a virtual synecdoche for the local temperament. I wouldn't quarrel with the spirit of this association even today. The original music and words were composed by Col. Sandford C. Faulkner (1808–1856). The primary document is not extant, but an 1876 arrangement by the colonel was published. The gist of it is well known: a wayfarer stops at a cabin in need of refuge. The squatter is on the porch fiddling the first half of a tune known as "The Arkansas Traveler." He continuously evades and breaks off the traveler's questions by repeating the tune's beginning. It finally occurs to the traveler to ask why the fiddler never finishes the score, and for the first time he nabs the squatter's attention. When the traveler shows him the turn of the tune, the squatter offers him every hospitality. In addition to the eleven distinct versions published by 1926, Masterson describes four credible ascriptions to the original besides Colonel Faulkner. Certain authorship is slippery; partial precedents and parallels are abundant in literature and lore. Throughout the latter part of the nineteenth century, "The Arkansas Traveler" manifested itself as minstrel song, ballad, skit, painting, lithograph, and a five-act play, which enjoyed a thirty-year run. As recently as 1981, folklorist W. K. McNeil chronicled the tune; Liz Parkhurst published a prose adaptation for children in 1982. Charles Albright's column by the same name in the *Democrat-Gazette* licenses the journalist to arkansas, daily, as he sees fit. Michelle Shocked's 1992 compact disc *The Arkansas Traveler* features a player monikered Arkansas Traveler on guitar, mandolin, and vocals and noted Arkansas songwriters and musicians, including Levon Helm and Jimmy Driftwood, thus carrying the icon into a new technology.

The flood of 1927 was another "master" subject. The first to ficitonalize it may have been Tennessee writer T. S. Tribling in *Backwater* (1930). One of countless personal accounts of the flood was vividly recorded by the mother of Indian poet Geary Hobson (b. 1941). His mother's family lived in Desha County near the confluence of the Arkansas and Mississippi Rivers. From the nine-year-old's perspective (her age at the time), a month spent as a refugee on the levee berm was a circumstance which brought everyone more or less happily together—family, friends, unwelcome strangers, and antipathetic critters alike: "I recall . . . seeing a short log float by with a small red rooster that seemed frozen with fear on one end and on the other end, sharing the log, was a large coiled rattlesnake."[16] The cautionary message the joining waters transmitted to her son would be to eschew summoning disaster:

> I come from a wet land
> (bayous hills old stomp-dance
> grounds flood-plain delta)
> and I never learned to sing for rain.[17]

"For My Brother and Sister Southwestern Indian Poets"

The Man in Black, singer/songwriter Johnny Cash, was born in Kingsland a few years too late to witness the flood of 1927, but not for the one of 1937. Cash grew up on that low cotton land in Dyess Colony, an experimental cooperative started by the Works Project Administration, and he scored one of his earliest hits in 1959 with "Five Feet High and Rising," in which the family's evacuation in a homemade boat becomes imminent, foot by foot, verse by verse. The central character of Henry Dumas's unfinished epic *Jonoah and the Green Stone* (1976) re-creates the flood of 1937; Jonoah is named, marked, and defined by it.

No one fictionalized the flood of 1927 more dramatically or, for that matter, with more painful accuracy than Richard Wright (1908–1960). "The Man Who Saw the Flood" (originally published as "Silt" in the *New Masses,* 1937) and "Down by the Riverside" (collected in *Uncle Tom's Children,* 1938) were published years after the author had left the Arkansas delta, but he was living in

Memphis at the time of the flood. Wright concentrated on the disproportionate suffering of black people during a natural disaster: the conscription of black labor, the losses of life and property, the increased level of violence whites directed against blacks during the disaster, and the forced return of tenants to landowners. By the powers vested in his art, he stripped the propaganda of goodwill between the races to the grimmer facts, and he vivified the rising waters with unstoppable energy.

An early anthology of Arkansas poets (1908) was collected by Bernie Babcock (1868–1962) from Russellville, a strong, skillful woman. A twenty-seven-year-old widow in 1897, with five small children underfoot, she made her living and her reputation as a suffragist, prohibitionist, newspaper and magazine editor, and novelist. She founded and directed Arkansas's Museum of Natural History; she was the folklore editor and state director of the Federal Writers Project. Under the aegis of the Federal Writers Project, Babcock oversaw an oral history survey, including personal interviews with over a thousand former slaves. Up to twenty local interviewers canvassed Arkansas. According to journalist Bob Lancaster, two of the interviewers were up to the task: Samuel S. Taylor, a black man from Little Rock, and Irene Robertson, a white woman from Hazen. Of the seventeen volumes retrieved and collected at the Library of Congress, the Arkansas interviews are the most comprehensive, a four-volume compilation of close to twenty-five hundred pages. Lancaster writes that the *Narratives* "make up one of our most moving documents—a true horror story, full of lasting hurt and an old rage, told mostly in a meditative strophe and antistrophe of blue funk."[18] Considerable credit is due to Babcock for ensuring that the state of Arkansas went on record on a profound scale.

Bernie Babcock wrote over forty novels, a number on Abe Lincoln and family, integrating much primary source material gathered from correspondence with junior staffers of the president and members of his wife's family. The first in the Lincoln series, *The Soul of Ann Rutledge* (1919), was reprinted fourteen times and translated several times over. The writing brings inflated significance to the old adjective, *sentimental*. However, Babcock not only supported her family with her prolific pen, she fought tooth and toenail for her convictions. In the fifties she retired to Petit Jean Mountain, where she died at ninety-four, a manuscript opened across her knees.[19]

Juvenile writer Charlie May Simon (1897–1977) began publishing in the thirties. She was born in the Ozarks. After studying at the Chicago Art Institute and under Bourdelle in Paris, she would choose the hills again. As late as 1952 Randolph rated her Ozark book, *Straw in the Sun* (New York: Dutton, 1945), her best work. It is rightly compared to Marjorie Kinnan Rawlings's *Cross Creek*. (In the film adaptation of *Cross Creek,* the lead was played by Arkansas actor Mary Steenburgen.) Both *Straw in the Sun* and *Cross Creek* are essentially the daybooks of writers looking for a home. Charlie May Simon chose, or was chosen by, Rocky Crossing, sixty acres of Ozark wilderness. In subsequent years, she wrote able biographies of Albert Schweitzer, de Chardin, Martin Buber, Toyohiko Kagawa, Andrew Carnegie, and Dag Hammarskjold for young readers. In 1972 she published *Razorbacks Are Really Hogs*. Charlie May Simon was the daughter of Wayman Hogue, who wrote so clearly about the backwoods, and wife of the tormented John Gould Fletcher.

A Little Rock poet whose work created a brief, bright blip with several collections was Karle Wilson Baker (1878–1960). She published *Blue Smoke* (1919), *The Garden of the Plynck* (1920), *Burning Bush* (1922), and *Old Coins* (1923) in the fledgling Yale Series of Younger Poets. She came from Little Rock, was educated at the University of Chicago, and later moved to Texas.

Some Fellow-Poets

> I love to see them sitting solemnly,
> Holding their souls like watches to their ears
> And shouting, every time they tick, "A Poem!"[20]

Neither watches nor poems tick anymore, but she had her time, and it is heartening to think of her and fellow poets keeping company early in the century.

Welcome the advent of the literature of the thirties: Vance Randolph (1892–1980) finally reaped the yield of his first decade of folklore collecting with the publication of *The Ozarks: An American Survival of Primitive Society* by Vanguard Press in 1931. Van Buren County's Wayman Hogue published his straightforward chronicle *Back Yonder* in 1932, a book Randolph was still boostering as the best nonfiction written about the Ozark country twenty years later. In 1947 John Gould Fletcher dedicated his state history to Hogue as the "true chronicler of the Arkansas backwoods." Fayetteville writer Charles Morrow Wilson (1905–1977) launched a sustained career in nonfiction as well as fiction with the novel *Acres of Sky* (1930), set near Hogeye, where former *New York Times* journalist Roy Reed tied off the nomadic leg of his career in the late 1970s.

Charles Morrow Wilson grew up on a farm outside of Fayetteville and began his writing career as a newspaperman. Journalism sent him globetrotting, but he remained expert on matters rural. By the age of twenty, he had been convinced that food supply was the premier determinant of behavior. "A man has got to eat so as to peck apples so as to make money so as to buy food stuffs for to feed hisself so as he can peck mo' apples,"[21] a migrant picker told the rookie journalist at a crossroads store in the Ozarks. He did not forget to repeat this Sisyphean bit of wisdom twenty-two books later. Hunger studies riveted his attention for the better part of his writing life, and neither history, nor statistics, nor his own witnessing deterred him from believing a more beneficent society was feasibly available to us. Incidentally, the gospel-according-to-Randolph ranks Wilson tops with respect to his use of dialect.

In 1920 a versatile English writer, Charles J. Finger, settled on a farm near Fayetteville, where he wrote a book on Confucius, a book on Mark Twain, frontier ballads, and a slew of romantic adventure tales. His *Tales from the Silver Lands* won the Newberry Prize for juvenile fiction in 1933. It was Randolph's expert opinion, however, that the polyglot was not attuned to the nuances of American dialect.[22]

Another wanderer whose work is rootbound to the state is John Gould Fletcher (1886–1950). Largely due to the magazines in which he originally published and the ex-pats he hung with, Amy Lowell and company, he was identified as an Imagist. True enough, he was pitched to the clearly defined image, pitched against rhetoric, and into the emotions of rhythm, but he was too wordy, emotive, and digressive for that taut scene. In the end Fletcher would refuse inclusion in *Des Imagistes,* "not wanting," he wrote the editor Harriet Monroe in 1913, "to be hampered with Mr. Pound's technique and his don'ts."[23] He was later linked with the Agrarian movement in literature, the Fugitive poets. He shared their adversarial relation to The Machine, and their old pride in the Old South, but Fletcher was changeful, ponderously religious, unstable, symbolistic, and finally unassimilable. He did not readily find his company, and he did not discover his regional strengths until late into the exploration of his own signature. His reputation suffered in part from his infidelity to any single tendency; his poetry remained exploratory. By the time he published his autobiography (1937), he had sent a dozen collections out into the world. In 1938 he won the Pulitzer for his *Selected Poems*. He authored books on Paul Gauguin and on John Smith and Pocahontas. Fletcher wrote an informal but substantive state history, first published in 1947 (reprinted, University of Arkansas Press, 1989). One inspired evening in Vance Randolph's living room, Fletcher created the Ozark Folklore Society, but he drowned himself in a stock pond the following year. Randolph succeeded him as president of the society.[24]

The heavyweight critics of Fletcher's prime took his poetry quite seriously. William Dean Howells, Mark Van Doren, and R. P. Blackmur wrote on his work, though the latter demoted it. Fletcher fell out with Pound, in part for criticizing his work, but Pound's review—of two books which Fletcher self-published and later self-dismissed—was generous, considering the source: "Mr. Fletcher has a fine crop of faults—mostly his own. He has such distinction as belongs to a man who dares to have his own faults, who prefers his own to those of anyone else . . . It is enough that I have read *The Dominant City* and *Fool's Gold* without being bored to death, without being choked on gobbets of sham Keats, and on fricasseed Francis Thompson."[25] Poet Amy Lowell praised the poetry for several thousand sentences without much focus; poet H. D. praised succinctly, especially for his handling of suggestion in spite of the Imagist stance on precision. The psychoanalytical Conrad Aiken thought Fletcher at his best when he went on nerve; otherwise not so good. An early posthumous consideration by Eugene Haun perceived Fletcher's poetry as burdened by a "peculiarly Protestant pessimism which causes more torment than all other kinds put together."[26] Haun thought him a major poet who had failed to achieve an effectual form. Several years later, comparative literature scholar Ben Kimpel undertook an essay of Fletcher's achievement for Harriet Monroe's *Poetry,* the longest-running poetry journal in the country. Professor Kimpel recognized Fletcher's principal technical failure as rhythmic, "broken-winded" to use Kimpel's term. He also rapped Fletcher's inability to stop when the poem begged to cease and desist. Fletcher's prose, with the exception of his autobiography, he considered excellent. In the final analysis, Kimpel perceived the poet as "almost the first strong intellectual force to which Arkansas had been exposed."[27] The qualifying "almost" is essential. There was Sequoyah, although visionary might be more descriptive of the force to which the Cherokee exposed Arkansas. Vance Randolph thought Fletcher "was a godamn fool, but . . . a great man somehow."[28] Whatever, the poet from Little Rock was our first modernist, and we were due one. What he brought back to the state—the news from abroad, French Symbolism, Taoism, even his angst, enlarged us, poets and non-poets alike. The cosmopolitan came back with a new regard for his native province, its past, and its promise. He brought with him the continuing and, for him, costly struggle for excellence in the old and doomed sense of the word:

> Set stone here to stone,
> Till this be made my own;
> Join wood to wood,
> See that the work be made good.
> Keep many trees
> So that my heart may find ease;
> Here in this shaken wood of days,
> May I, of my desire,
> Await the ebbing of earth's offered fire.
> —from "The Land Is Cleared"[29]

Aesthetically antipodal to Fletcher is activist poet Don West (b. 1907). In his brilliant argument *Repression and Recovery: Modern American Poetry and Politics of the Cultural Memory, 1910–1945*, critic Cary Nelson cites the Fayetteville writer thus: "When West was publishing in the *New Masses* and *The Daily Worker* in the 1930s thousands of people had contact with his work; thousands of people thereby recognized the existence of a radical southern literary tradition . . . a tradition largely forgotten now that agrarians are taken to represent the South."[30] West's first collection of poems, modestly if invasively titled *Crab-Grass,* appeared in 1931. Don West's autobiographical novel *Broadside to the Sun* quietly measures the isolated struggles of the individual against the parameters of freedom, against the natural order, against the pressures of the dominant model: "Why shouldn't I go on carrying cream to town the slow way? If they didn't take me into the army . . ."[31]

Vance Randolph was born in Pittsburg, Kansas, in 1892, six years after John Gould Fletcher; they were to be friends, but Randolph lived a very different life. Randolph created a very different *oeuvre*, and he lived long enough to see its influence begin to take root and grow. The reputation was a long time coming. His great labor was deep into its maturity. He was confined to Sunset Manor, a nursing home in Fayetteville, when I was a graduate student at the

University of Arkansas. On the evenings young folklorists Michael Luster and Robert Cochran were keeping his incredible company, I was likely slouched in a booth arguing with one of my belligerent betters at George's Majestic Lounge, the bar where my father used to down an occasional brew on the eve of World War II. Randolph, at the end of the seventies, was bounded by the same city limits, bedridden but otherwise himself, writ large. *Pissing in the Snow* came out in 1976. It was the only book I knew by Randolph at the time. Randolph died in 1980.

Randolph, the "compleat folklorist," was not unschooled; he was untrained. He schooled at Kansas State University and Clark University, where he got a master's in psychology. He trained himself. After a brief layover in New York City, he found work in Kansas, writing for the Socialist weekly, *Appeal to Reason*. He wrote a slew of Little Blue Books for Haldeman-Julius. He was in training. He trained himself as an expert ghost, writing booklets on physiology, bees, and dreams, and writing crambooks—the ABCs of chemistry, evolution, biology, physiology, psychology, geology. He wrote dictionaries in French and German. He wrote *German Self-Taught*. He ghosted and ghost-edited a slew of confessionals, successfully passing himself off in print as a madame, a pimp, a virgin, a rapist, an abortionist, a ghost writer, and a booze fighter. Only the latter two were tainted by autobiography. He ghosted a book on etiquette. He published a couple of academic papers on butterflies, for he might have become a lepidopterist. He wrote for outdoor magazines. He was avid. He studied Yiddish, off and on, for years. He contracted out as an MGM hack, but that was to be a short-lived source of income, for he held to a different standard of authenticity than they did in the hills of Hollywood.

The hack work kept the wolf away. Randolph had already published a study on regional speech by 1926. He was already collecting "The Songs Grandfather Sang" through a weekly column he edited in Pineville, Missouri. He was already harvesting his wife's tales. He was interested in the entire: songs, tall tales, jokes, riddles, superstitions, wisecracks, dialect. The field was his. He was nearly fifty before a recorder was sent by the Library of Congress. The songs alone fill four volumes. These are the folklife books: *The Ozarks, Ozark Mountain Folks, An Ozark Anthology, Ozark Folksongs, Ozark Superstitions, We Always Lie to Strangers, Who Blowed Up the Church House, Down in the Holler, The Devil's Pretty Daughter, The Talking Turtle, Sticks in the Knapsack, Hot Springs and Hell, Ozark Folklore: A Bibliography, Pissing in the Snow,* and *Roll Me in Your Arms* and *Blow*

18

the Candle Out, two volumes of "unprintable Ozark folk songs and folklore." These are fiction: *From an Ozark Holler, The Camp on Wildcat Creek, Hedwig.* This is what he was doing during the Great War (though he served, after a fashion, in a VA hospital), what he did during the Great Depression, and what he did during the next war as well. When the field was young and codifying its strategies from inside the academy, Randolph was pioneering on the outside. He was nearly sixty when awarded an honorary degree, seventy when he married for love, and eighty-six when elected a Fellow of the American Folklore Society. But the sweetest reward, for the stranger, the reader, is that the work is wonderful. He was fluent in his medium; he was compleat.

Once poet laureate of the state, Rosa Marinoni (1888–1970) lived in Fayetteville. During the more than twenty years John Gould Fletcher spent as an exile in Europe, the Italian-born poet was marrying into the Arkansas intelligentsia. She was an activist for relief and suffrage. She published a number of poetry collections, beginning with *Behind the Mask* in 1927, and was at her level best when she transcribed the quotidian, "grass covering her run-down heels";[32] she was at her worst when formulating the sublime, "climbing steps that led into beauty and winding stairs that led into pain."[33] A new selection of the thirties' poets would create an interesting addition to the record of the time, perhaps a more unsparing and, at the same time, a sparer one (poetry being bent on an irreducible language) than much of the prose tends to foreground.

At least one sacred songwriter of the thirties would necessarily be included in any anthology of the decade, Albert E. Brumley (1905–1977), whose best lyrics and melodies were written during the Depression, songs such as: "I'll Fly Away" (1932), "I'll Meet You in the Morning" (1936), "Jesus, Hold My Hand" (1938), "Turn Your Radio On" (1938), and "I Found a Hiding Place" (1939). Brumley's enrollment at Eugene M. Bartlett's Music Institute in 1926, in the coal-mining town of Hartford, Arkansas, would commence a harmonious creative partnership with Bartlett and mark the career beginnings of a major Ozark contributor to gospel songwriting. Dozens of Brumley's nearly seven hundred songs have been offered as "sugar sticks" at concerts and singing conventions; they have been published, recorded, re-recorded, and permanently posited in the repertoires of quartets and congregations throughout the country.[34] Any aperture created for songwriters of the period would also focus in on blues artist Peetie Wheatstraw (William Bunch, 1902–1941), who grew up in Cotton Plant and recorded over a hundred and sixty sides between 1930 and 1941, including many original lyrics such as "Bring Me Flowers While I'm Living," "Don't Hang My Clothes on No Barb Wire Line," "Good Whiskey Blues," "Possum Den Blues," and "Throw Me in the Alley." Known as the High Sheriff of Hell and also as the Devil's Son-in-Law, Wheatstraw's graphically sexual and frequently violent lines could not have been penned at a greater remove from Brumley's inspirations. Such distant orientations, synchronically in play, point to the range of expressions required to cope with the times when, as Brumley said, "the poor had no time at all." And one would have difficulty reconciling either Brumley's or Wheatstraw's language to the lyrics of Pinkley Tomlin of Eros (b. 1908), whose popular "The Object of My Affection" was a 1934 smash.

Before the thirties were over, C. Vann Woodward's doctoral thesis, *Tom Watson, Agrarian Rebel,* was published, and it was still in print in 1975. In Tom Watson, Woodward saw the embodiment of the paradoxical extremes of southern politics of the 1890s: insurrection and demogoguery. In the figure of one man Woodward saw the personal, class, and sectional tragedy of the South's possibility side by side with its shame. In Woodward, of Vanndale (b. 1908), the country raised its preeminent scholar of the South and its most literary historical voice. In Woodward, there is no conflict between the demands of intellectual analysis and the authority of style. This is why you will find the better part of his books in print—from the Watson biography published in 1938 to the *Old World's New World,* 1991. This is why it was possible for a dyed-in-the-blue-blazer academic to produce a popular study (*The Strange Career of Jim Crow,* 1955) and to take home a Pulitzer (*Mary Chesnut's Civil War,* 1981).

Lily Peter, another poet laureate of the state, was born in the Delta in 1891. Her central literary preoccupation would be with the state's number-one conquistador, De Soto. Her first collection of poems would not appear until the 1960s. She had the time. Lily Peter would live until 1991. The long span of her life encircles the careers of all but the youngest writer in this selection, Pat Phillips, who is just beginning to publish.

All of these writers, Lily Peter included, are contemporary, down-home writers. Among them are the highborn, the monied, the schooled-in-the-East; the offspring of preachers, teachers, and scribblers; also the poor, the self-taught. All of them qualify. All of them arkansas.

For the purpose of this project, the designation Arkansas writer remains generous. In the main, a writer who has spent a significant period of time in the state can claim or be claimed by the state. For the sake of limits, individual writers whose stay was defined by college attendance are excluded. Departed or exiled native sons and daughters who spent their formative years in the state have been included. So have transplants. For the most part my focus is upon poets, fiction writers, and belletrists; that is, writers for whom aesthetic values are essential, even primary. At the same time, the customary literary genre distinctions have been overruled when a song lyric or even a recipe claimed synonymous attention. The goal is to provide Arkansas and its visitors with a prideful sense of what has been written and what is being written here by means of the concepts and rhythms of art.

Notes

1. Bob Lancaster, *The Jungles of Arkansas: A Personal History of the Wonder State* (Fayetteville: University of Arkansas Press, 1989), 29.

2. Henry Rowe Schoolcraft, *A View of the Lead Mines of Missouri, 1819* (Salem, N.H.: Arno Press, Inc.; reprint ed., 1972), 261–62.

3. Workers of the Writers' Program of the Works Projects Administration in the State of Arkansas, compilation, *Arkansas: A Guide to the State* (New York: Hastings House, 1941), 156. *The WPA Guide to 1930s Arkansas* (Lawrence: University Press of Kansas, reprint ed., 1987). See also Thomas Nuttall, *Journal of Travels into the Arkansas Territory, 1819* (Philadelphia: T. H. Palmer, 1821; Norman: University of Oklahoma, reprint, 1979).

4. *Arkansas: A Guide to the State,* 157. See also George W. Featherston-haugh, *Excursion through the Slave States . . . with Sketches of Popular Manners and Geological Notices* (London: John Murray, 1844). Refers to travels of 1834.

5. Grant Foreman, *Sequoyah* (Norman: University of Oklahoma Press, 1938), 28–29.

6. Ibid., 69.

7. James R. Masterson, *Tall Tales of Arkansas* (Boston: Chapman and Grimes, Inc., 1943), 29–54.

8. Ibid., 32–33.

9. Ibid., 57.

10. Ibid.

11. Vance Randolph, *Down in the Holler: A Gallery of Ozark Folk Speech* (Norman: University of Oklahoma Press, 1953; third printing, 1986), 125.

12. Ethel C. Simpson, ed., *Simpkinsville and Vicinity: Arkansas Stories of Ruth McEnery Stuart* (Fayetteville: University of Arkansas Press, 1983), 7.

13. J. H. Smith, *Maudelle: A Novel Founded on Facts Gathered from Living Witnesses* (Boston: Mayhew Publishing Co., 1906), preface.

14. Ibid.

15. Octavius Coke, ed., *Scrapbook of Arkansas Literature* (American Caxton Society Press, 1939), 156.

16. Edythe Simpson Hobson, "Twenty-Seven Days on the Levee," *Arkansas Historical Quarterly* 39 (Autumn 1980): 215.

17. Geary Hobson, *Deer Hunting and Other Poems* (New York and Norman, Okla.: Strawberry Press with Renegade/Point Riders Press, 1990), 21.

18. Lancaster, *The Jungles of Arkansas,* 109.

19. Marcia Camp, "The Soul of Bernie Babcock," *Pulaski County Historical Review* 36 (Fall 1988): 62.

20. Karle Baker Wilson, *Blue Smoke* (New Haven, Conn.: Yale University Press, 1919), 95.

21. Charles Morrow Wilson, *The Fight against Hunger* (New York: Funk and Wagnalls, 1969), 3.

22. Randolph, *Down in the Holler,* 132.

23. Paula Kepos, ed., *Twentieth-Century Literary Criticism,* vol. 35 (Detroit: Gale Research, Inc., 1990), 103. Stanley K. Coffman Jr., *Imagism: A Chapter for the History of Modern Poetry* (Norman: University of Oklahoma Press, 1951), 175–76.

24. Robert Cochran, *Vance Randolph: An Ozark Life* (Urbana and Chicago: University of Illinois Press, 1985), 202.

25. Kepos, *Twentieth-Century Literary Criticism,* 35:90. Ezra Pound, "In Metre," *The New Freewoman* 7 (1913): 131–32.

26. Kepos, *Twentieth-Century Literary Criticism,* 35:99. Eugene Haun, "Of Broken Effort and Desire: A General Consideration of the Poetry of John Gould Fletcher," *Shenandoah* 2 (Spring 1951): 3–16.

27. Kepos, *Twentieth-Century Literary Criticism,* 35:106. Ben Kimpel, "John Gould Fletcher in Retrospect," *Poetry* 69 (August 1954): 284–96.

28. Cochran, *Vance Randolph,* 202.

29. John Gould Fletcher, *The Burning Mountain* (New York: E. P. Dutton, 1946), 65.

30. Cary Nelson, *Repression and Recovery: Modern American Poetry and Politics of the Cultural Memory, 1910–1945* (Madison: University of Wisconsin Press, 1989), 166.

31. Don West, *Broadside to the Sun* (New York: W. W. Norton and Company, 1946), 203.

32. Coke, *Scrapbook of Arkansas Literature,* 105.

33. Ibid., 218.

34. Kay Hively and Albert E. Brumley Jr., *I'll Fly Away: The Life Story of Albert E. Brumley* (Branson, Mo.: Mountaineer Books, 1990).

Writers

Living in Little Rock
with Miss Little Rock

Once, a long time ago, the trees were as vital as you pretend to be. They were intelligent, aware. They spoke among themselves in chemicals on the wind. They feasted on what was nearly the body of God, the light of the sun itself. They had neither mouths nor eyes, but they had a thing that was both and neither: they exfoliated. They were fluid, they sang, they grew, they danced. In fact, they still and always do, if you have eyes that are slow enough to see, ears that are tuned low and frail enough to hear. It is true that their intelligence was a more distributed intelligence than yours, and it is true that they died where they grew, but when has that ever contradicted a dance? As fine as it was to be a tree, however, there was sin among trees. They starved each other for the light, the tall shadowing out the young without regard to grace or form, size and power the only consideration. And though they were mono- and dioecious, and floated ther delicious sexuality on the air, and all together came in every spring, and all together bore fruit every fall, so that there was no such thing as infidelity, they yet discovered how to betray, and how to lie. As punishment for their sins (this is the story the trees tell), God made a sort of whizzing invisible ghost, a sort of rootless unhappy demon moving too fast to recognize, whose function it was to torture and strip and mutilate, to force the trees into a rigid and geometrical death, or to breed them into unknown forms. But then God had pity and sent a Tree of Trees, a slender and perfect youngling without a flaw. Smooth she was on the wind, and prettily she ate the light. She told of a tree of stars, and made her life an image of what she told. Soon her fame had drifted over the world. Of course this could not be permitted. The elders, dark with struggle, the bitterly twisted survivors, they realized they must deal with this most false and dangerous of hopes. And so it was that a human was found (for that is what they were, those fastforward spooks, that blurring branching of hatchets) and drawn into its fate, as trees know how to draw things to themselves: and the Tree of Trees was cut down and crossed upon herself, and fastened to a man to die.

Jack Butler

About A Year After He Got Married
He Would Sit Alone In An Abandoned
Shack In A Cotton Field
Enjoying Himself

I'd sit inside the abandoned shack all morning
Being sensitive, a fair thing to do
At twenty-three, my first son born, and burning
To get my wife again. The world was new
And I was nervous and wonderfully depressed.

The light on the cotton flowers and the child
Asleep at home was marvelous and blessed,
And the dust in the abandoned air was mild
As sentimental poverty. I'd scan
Or draw the ragged wall on the morning long.

Newspaper for wallpaper sang but didn't mean.
Hard thoughts of justice were beyond my ken.
Lord, forgive young men their gentle pain,
Then bring them stones. Bring their play to ruin.

James Whitehead

Womenfolks

My mother and the other women I knew as a
child were farm women, one or two generations
removed from the real pioneer days, gentled and
domesticated by the time I came among them.
But the marks were there. Their skins were leath-
ery from working outdoors. Some of these wom-
en were serene and some, hot-tempered, and in
either case they brooked no transgressions of
their notions of morality, and woe to the mortal
who spoke to these women with disrespect. They
were not innocent or submissive or delicately
constituted, nor afraid of balky cows or chicken
hawks. It took them approximately two hours to
transform a live rooster into Sunday dinner.
They could reason with a mule and shoot a gun.
But they also knew just how to take hold of a
baby and what to say to a weeping two-year-old.
I used to hang on the backs of their chairs as they
peeled peaches by the bushel and talked about
how to keep dill pickle jars from exploding and
why Cousin Rosity had got the cancer she was
dying from, and what effect the drought would
have on cattle prices, and how the doctors had
decided to cut off poor Uncle Jules' leg ("Orght
to be ashamed of themselves, him being ninety
and about dead anyhow of that diabetes"), but
danged if the old man hadn't got up off his bed
and run them out of his house. Sometimes, thinking the children out of earshot, or perhaps deem-
ing us old enough to hear, they would forget their
ironclad morals and recount some scandal that
was simmering in a cottage down the road a piece
or even tell a bawdy joke. Never anything explic-
it, merely the gropings of newlyweds, forever
doomed to get the vaseline mixed up with the
glue. In later years, when I was adolescent, it
shocked me to hear them laugh out loud about
such things. How could they joke about anything
so awesome? Had they no sense of romance?
Then when the peaches were peeled and sliced
into half a dozen enamel dishpans, they would
make me stand at a tub of scalding, soapy water
and wash out Kerr-Mason jars by the case. It took
a child's hand for that. Theirs were too splayed.
I have watched those knobby brown fingers lay-
ing French plaits into my cousin June's black
hair, my own being too fuzzy to braid, and I have
known those women to walk five miles to spend
an afternoon at a quilting frame. It never oc-
curred to me then that they were carriers and
conservators of a culture of their own, one that
I would have to unravel one day and reknit.

Shirley Abbott

Going Back Home

Sometimes I wonder   why did I ever leave home
Sometimes I wonder   why'd I ever leave home

I had a few dollars in my pocket
Ooh   now that little change is gone

I didn't think a city   Whoa could be so doggone mean
I didn't think a city   Boy could be so doggone mean

Ah but this is the meanest place   hahaha
Lord I've ever seen

I used to have a job   doing spot labor every day
I used to have a job   doing spot labor every day

But when I got to work this morning
Lord they'd packed up and move away

I called my boss   Well I want to know can I come back home
Yes I called my boss   I want to know can I come back home

He said Nah, you know sorry Son, haha
Boy your house is gone

Mmmmhmm   Where in the world am I going to do
Mmmmhmm   Where in the world am I gonna be

I guess it's just all wrapped up in a nutshell now
Oh it look like old pro Son is through

Son Seals

Deep Blues

The significance of Delta blues is often thought to be synonymous with its worldwide impact. According to this line of reasoning, the music is important because some of the world's most popular musicians—the Rolling Stones, Bob Dylan, Eric Clapton—learned to sing and play by imitating it and still revere the recorded works of the Delta masters. It's important because rock guitarists everywhere play with a metal or glass slider on their fingers, a homage, acknowledged or not, to Delta musicians like Muddy Waters and Elmore James. It's important because Delta guitarists were the first on records to deliberately explore the uses of feedback and distortion. It's important because almost everyone who picks up a harmonica, in America or England or France or Scandinavia, will at some stage in his development emulate either Little Walter or a Little Walter imitator. It's important because bass patterns, guitar riffs, and piano boogies invented in the Delta course through a broad spectrum of Western popular music, from hard rock to singer-songwriter pop to disco to jazz to movie soundtracks. It's important because Delta bluesmen like Muddy Waters and Robert Johnson have become icons, larger-than-life figures who seem to have articulated some of contemporary America's highest aspirations and darkest secrets with incomparable immediacy in music they made thirty or forty years ago. ❦ These are all good reasons for listening to and learning about Delta blues, but they're neither the only reasons nor the best reasons. The music has never needed interpreters or popularizers; it's always been strong enough to stand on its own. Its story, from the earliest shadowy beginnings to the Chicago migration to the present worldwide popularity of Muddy Waters and some younger Delta-born bluesmen, is an epic as noble and as essentially American as any in our history. It's the story of a small and deprived group of people who created, against tremendous odds, something that has enriched us all.

Robert Palmer

34

36

Heaved From The Earth

after the tornado, a dead moccasin
nailed to the pole
boards scattered across a pasture

lying fierce crosses
jagged in mud

had flung itself
nail and wood
the square-head animal
hurled also in air

or as it raced in weeds
)water flowing, water falling
impaled

      both the snake and timber
went flying through with wind

coiled, made a coil (they do
immediately from danger or when hurt
and died in a coil
bit itself
in pain of its own defense the poison

      birds
      hurled into yard
      fences
      one with feet tangled gripping
      the open wire, a big jay
struggling from the water
throwing its fanged head
high at the lightning, silent
in all that thunder

to die by its own mouth
pushing the fire thorns in

Besmilr Brigham

Born In The Delta

Barns and cribs to play in have been the salvation of many a lonely country child, but in addition to these, we had, within fifty yards of our back door, a living, seething swamp for our personal entertainment. It never seemed to occur to anyone that it might not be a good idea to let small children play in a swamp infested with thousands of poisonous snakes, possibly because snakes were so much a part of the scenery that nobody paid them any mind. I have never seen them in such concentration in any other place except the snake house at the St. Louis zoo. They were swimming or sunning themselves on logs and tree limbs everywhere you looked in that swamp. When I was very young there was a rotten old scow around that the older boys had built, and before we got in it, we were careful to chase out the cottonmouth moccasins that liked to hide under the seats. We also had to be careful about paddling under overhanging limbs, because in their fright snakes had been known to roll off into the boat. ❧ Some of those snakes were four feet long and three inches thick. Moccasins are extremely shy, however, and we learned early that they were as scared of us as we might be of them. A good chicken game was to see who could let an unsuspecting snake swim closest to a bare foot dangling down the bank to the edge of the water. The closest I could stand to let one come to my foot was about twenty-four inches. You sat very still until you couldn't bear it getting any closer and then all you had to do was twitch your foot and the terrified snake would rise straight up and fall over backwards getting away. We believed that they would not bite under water. Whether true or not, this idea was comforting, because there were times when the boat sank or we were gigging frogs or something and absolutely had to be in the water ourselves. None of the children ever got bitten playing in the swamp. Ironically, the only person in the family ever to suffer snakebite was Mother, who was mortally afraid of them anyway. One day before I was born, she put her hand under a sweet-potato vine in the garden and a rattlesnake bit it. There was nobody home to take her to the doctor. The only person near was an old woman who grabbed a chicken and cut it open alive and told Mother to stick her hand in the warm body of the dying chicken "to draw out the poison." Apparently it did; the hand swelled to twice its normal size and mother was sick for a few days, but that was the end of it.

Margaret Jones Bolsterli

The Old World's New World

Nothing was simpler than access to the White House through most of the nineteenth century, and a presentation to the President was easy to arrange and startlingly informal. No guards at the gate, no sentries at the door, no police, no soldiers, no servants in livery, and the public rooms "as open to everybody as the reading rooms of a public library," according to a visitor in 1883. From the time of President Monroe to that of McKinley, White House receptions were crowded with citizens of varied ranks mixed with the highest federal officials, civil and military, along with ambassadors of the diplomatic corps. The last were conspicuous for clinging to the splendors of uniform, regalia, and decorations. The contrast they offered at the second inauguration of President McKinley in 1901 is described by one witness: a brilliant array of court uniforms, "Siam, Korea, Hungary, and Portugal as gay as butterflies," against sober American officials in broadcloth, "without a star, a ribbon, or a sword between them; the effect was almost comic." Foreigners encountered the same rule of accessibility, informality, and absence of ceremony up and down the ranks of officialdom, including cabinet ministers, generals, bishops, governors. A Norwegian was startled to be presented to the governor of a western state and recognize him as a man he had seen half an hour before in work clothes repairing his chimney. On enquiring for the governor of Arkansas at his home another foreigner was informed by the first lady of that state that his Excellency "was gone to the woods to hunt for a sow and pigs belonging to her..." Such experiences confirmed the opinion of foreign critics of the democracy that public office was not to be had without abandonment of dignity and that as a consequence the occupant of such office was deprived of authority and respect.

C. Vann Woodward

Bury My Heart At Wounded Knee

In the first seconds of violence, the firing of carbines was deafening, filling the air with powder smoke. Among the dying who lay sprawled on the frozen ground was Big Foot. Then there was a brief lull in the rattle of arms, with small groups of Indians and soldiers grappling at close quarters, using knives, clubs, and pistols. As few of the Indians had arms, they soon had to flee, and then the big Hotchkiss guns on the hill opened up on them, firing almost a shell a second, raking the Indian camp, shredding the tepees with flying shrapnel, killing men, women, and children.

When the madness ended, Big foot and more than half of his people were dead or seriously wounded; 153 were known dead, but many of the wounded crawled away to die afterward. One estimate placed the final total of dead at very nearly three hundred of the original 350 men, women, and children. The soldiers shot twenty-five dead and thirty-nine wounded, most of them struck by their own bullets or shrapnel.

After the wounded cavalrymen were started for the agency at Pine Ridge, a detail of soldiers went over the Wounded Knee battle-field, gathering up Indians who were still alive and loading them into wagons. As it was apparent by the end of the day that a blizzard was approaching, the dead Indians were left lying where they had fallen. (After the blizzard, when a burial party returned to Wounded Knee, they found the bodies, including Big Foot's frozen into grotesque shapes.)

The wagonloads of wounded Sioux (four men and forty-seven woman and children) reached Pine Ridge after dark. Because all available barracks were filled with soldiers, they were left lying in the open wagons in the bitter cold while an inept Army officer searched for shelter. Finally the Episcopal mission was opened, the benches taken out, and hay scattered over the rough flooring.
It was the fourth day after Christmas in the Year of Our Lord 1890.

When the first torn and bleeding bodies were carried into the candlelit church, those who were conscious could see Christmas greenery hanging from the open rafters. Across the chancel front above the pulpit was strung a crudely lettered banner; PEACE ON EARTH, GOOD WILL TO MEN.

Dee Brown

Pigs

It is not the wolf
but his howl in the hollow wind

they fear. His mouth is a great cave
and that howl the master of it—

that sound calling like the night,
calling what is dark to its vacant center.

Straw by straw, stick by stick,
brick by solid brick, there is no way

to keep that sound from entering.
But try. Move in together, give birth,

have other kinds of dreams. Sleep
with a light turned on, with cotton in your ears.

And by the evening fire tell the stories
of your ancestors. Tell how clever they were,

how they tempted the Devil from the skins
of the innocent. How they burned him

from those useless lives: Catholics, Jews,
witches, saints. And with fire like this.

With fire like this.

Andrea Hollander Budy

43

I Know Why The Caged Bird Sings

Until I was thirteen and left Arkansas for good, the Store was my favorite place to be. Alone and empty in the mornings, it looked like an unopened present from a stranger. Opening the front doors was pulling the ribbon off the unexpected gift. The light would come in softly (we faced north), easing itself over the shelves of mackerel, salmon, tobacco, thread. It fell flat on the big vat of lard and by noontime during the summer the grease had softened to a thick soup. Whenever I walked into the Store in the afternoon, I sensed that it was tired. I alone could hear the slow pulse of its job half done. But just before bedtime, after numerous people had walked in and out, had argued over their bills, or joked about their neighbors, or just dropped in "to give sister Henderson a 'Hi y'all'," the promise of magic mornings returned to the Store and spread itself over the family in washed life waves.

Momma opened boxes of crispy crackers and we sat around the meat block at the rear of the Store. I sliced onions and Bailey opened two or even three cans of sardines and allowed their juice of oil and fishing boats to ooze down and around the sides. That was supper. In the evening, when we were alone like that, Uncle Willie didn't stutter or shake or give any indication that he had an "affliction." It seemed that the peace of a day's ending was an assurance that the covenant God made with children, Negroes and the crippled was still in effect.

Maya Angelou

46

Some Other Place. The Right Place.

You will have wanted your dream to stick around, you will have hoped that that recapturing of the bright unlonely past would stay more, a little while, long enough for you to talk with your beloved firefly Lara again, but that dream, like all dreams, will pass away, and you will be left lying in bed remembering what will seem to have been, even more, a dream: the pressures and touches of Diana's arms and hands, the wrapping of the back of your neck in the crook of her elbow, the way her fingertips had clutched the small of your back, the clasp of her armpits on your shoulder and ribs, the clench of her clavicle on your throat....

You will spring out of bed, full of zest for the new day (not knowing, I'm sorry, that this will be your last day), and first you will search the wall to reassure yourself that my supreme prescription had not been a dream. Yes, it is still there in the daylight, that old-fashioned hand scrawling that injunction to embrace and cling and touch and hug and enfold and cuddle and squeeze and hold. Then you will notice (why it has taken you so long to notice my walls, old Gimleteye)? that all four of the white plaster walls are covered with pencilings; aphorisms, epigrams, sententious graffiti: observations on nature and on human nature, mottoes, reminders, lists: an old man talking to himself on his walls.

I'm not certain you will be quite ready for it, just then, but since it is your last day you will find my nine beatitudes:

Donald Harington

47

Walking After Supper

It is when I have thought of the universe
expanding until an atom becomes the size
of a solar system and millions of years pass
during the forming of a single thought,
of some place where gigantic young are taught
that we were here (though this will be known
by no evidence but logic alone,
all signs of us, and even our sun, gone),

that I have sometimes had to remind myself
that, say, if in a car at a crosswalk
a woman waves for me to go ahead,
this act deserves attention; that her doing that
equals in gravity all that has ever been
or will have been when we and the sun are dead.
All this I think in Fayetteville, Arkansas,
frozen here on the curb, in love, in awe.

Miller Williams
for Howard

Eyesight To The Blind

You're talking about your woman,
I wish to God, man that you could see mine;
you're talking about your woman,
I wish to God that you could see mine:
every time the little girls start to loving,
she bring eyesight to the blind.
Lord, her daddy must have been a millionaire,
'cause I can tell by the way she walk;
her daddy must have been a millionaire,
because I can tell by the way she walk:
Every time she start to loving,
the deaf and dumb begin to talk.

    I remember one Friday morning,
    we was lying down across the bed;
    man in the next room a-dying,
    stopped dying and lift up his head,
    and said, "Lord!
ain't she pretty,
and the whole
state know she fine."
Every time she start to loving,
she bring eyesight to the blind.
(All right and all right, now.
Lay it on me lay it on me lay it on me.
O lordy.
What a woman, what a woman!)
Yes, I declare she's pretty;
and the whole state knows she's fine.
Man, I declare she's pretty;
God knows I declare she's fine.
Every time she starts to loving, whoo!
She brings eyesight to the blind.
(I've got to get out of here, now.
Let's go, let's go, let's go now.)

Sonny Boy Williamson

What About This

A guy comes walking out of the garden
Playing Dark Eyes on the accordian.
We're sitting on the porch,
Drinking and spitting, lying.
We shut our eyes, snap our fingers.
Dewhurst goes out to his truck
Like he doesn't believe what he's seeing
And brings back three half-pints.
A little whirlwind occurs in the road,
Carrying dust away like a pail of water.
We're drinking serious now, and O.Z.
Wants to break in the store for some head cheese.
But the others won't let him.
Everybody laughs, dances.
The crossroads are all quiet
Except for the little man on the accordian.
Things are dying down, the moon spills its water.
Dewhurst says he smells rain.
O.Z. says if it rains he'll still make a crop.
We wait there all night, looking for rain.
We haven't been to sleep, so the blue lizards
On the side of the white porch
Lose their tails when we try to dream.
The man playing the music looks at us,
Noticing what we're up to. He backs off,
Holding up his hands in front, smiling,
Shaking his head, but before he gets half way
Down the road that O.Z. shoots him in the belly.
All summer his accordian rotted in the ditch,
Like an armadillo turning into a house payment.

Frank Stanford

Goodbye Sweetwater

"A mad dog will bite anybody, son. It don't matter who it used to belong to. It even bite the man what raised it. A mad dog will bite its own mother, son. So I'm sayin, son, be mad but not like a mad dog. Be right first. Be truthful first. And when you get mad at somethin then you got all that to back you up. Don't spite that man cause he thirsty and white. That's wrong. Give 'em your best at all times. When you give 'em your best when you don't like him, he be the first to know it. God on your side then." ❧ It never mattered whether he really agreed with Granny or not, because she seemed to be right. Mrs. Fields, in her silence, had only glanced at him, and he knew that she was backing up his grandmother. It was a conspiracy. It was a bond which he could not understand nor defeat, and nothing in his experience seemed full enough to satisfy him. His mother was not sending for him. She too was trapped. In the North she wasn't doing as good as she said. He had heard how that in cities up North they were having race riots and killing Negroes. Then what good was his trying to wait till she sent out Mr. Stubbs? There wasn't no man. His father was dead and that was it. He felt himself now ready to cast off the dreams and things people said. He would believe no one, and if he dreamed something, he would not believe it were true until he made it come true....If he were going to leave soon, then it would be because he wanted to. Even if his mother sent a ticket, it would mean nothing unless he wanted to leave. His grandmother would not drink sulfur water unless she had to and he knew that as long as there was sweet water coming out of the ground, she would be strong.... ❧ A long whistle broke the late evening heaviness, and Layton stopped packing his suitcase and went out to the bald yard... If he climbed the tree to see the passenger train, he knew that he would not fall.

Henry Dumas

Skillet-Sizzled Buttermilk Cornbread

This is the first Southern dish I learned how to fix, back when I was still a Yankee. (Of course, some—many—would say you never outgrow this handicap, no matter how long you live in the South.) Interestingly it is one of the most requested recipes at the inn and a house specialty: almost always on the menu. It is, to me, the perfect cornbread—in the mid to upper range of luxury among cornbreads, rich with eggs and buttermilk, slightly sweetened, buttery, very grainy. As often as I eat this, I never tire of it. An Amazing number of people have told me it was just like what their mother or grandmother used to make. And my old Arkansawyer pal Alan Leverett, founder of both the *Arkansas Times* and *Southern* magazines, claims it is the best he has ever eaten. But I learned how to make it in New York.

1 cup stone-ground yellow cornmeal
1 cup unbleached all-purpose flour
1 tablespoon baking powder
¼ teaspoon baking soda
1 ¼ cups buttermilk, preferably Bulgarian-style
1 large egg
2 to 4 tablespoons sugar
¼ cup mild vegetable oil, such as corn or peanut
Pam cooking spray
2 to 4 tablespoons butter

1. Preheat the oven to 375 F.

2. In a large bowl, combine the cornmeal, flour, baking powder, and salt.

3. In a small bowl, stir the baking soda into the buttermilk. In a second bowl, whisk together the egg, sugar to taste, and the oil, then whisk in the buttermilk.

4. Spray an 8- or 9-inch cast-iron skillet with Pam. Put the skillet over medium-high heat, add the butter, and heat until the butter melts and is just starting to sizzle. Tilt the pan to coat the bottom and sides.

5. Add the wet ingredients to the dry, and quickly stir together, using only as many strokes as needed to combine. Scrape the batter into the hot, buttery skillet. Immediately put the skillet in the oven and bake until golden brown, about 25 minutes. Cut into wedges to serve.

Thanks, Viola.

Crescent Dragonwagon

An Ozarker who doesn't like cornbread is said to have gone back on his raisin', which is almost as bad as denying one's kinfolks. An Arkansas governor, at a public dinner, was admonished, 'Don't go back on your raisin', Governor!' Whereupon the governor grinned, dropped the roll he had selected, and took a corn muffin instead.-
Vance Randolph

56

The Stump

When they lost the farm near Omaha
and their money,
the farmer's wife thought of it
as losing an arm.
The stump was a challenge.
It was, she said,
for the time being.
A healthy arm would sprout
if she were patient and wise and a hard worker.
But the stump healed smooth.
She watched things disappear:
the TV, the car, her teeth,
and still the stump offered nothing.
One night she began to understand
it would be with her always,
mean as a pig.

Jo McDougall

Hunting The Old Iron

Once upon a time a man went out into a big, dark, dense forest. He had his dogs with him, and his rifle, because he was hunting the old iron. He went deeper and deeper into the woods. Finally, way up in the top of a big oak tree he seen the old iron. And he called the dogs: "Hyar, Shep! Hyar, Tray! Hyar, Bruce! Hyar, Rover! Hyar, Caesar! Hyar, Ring! Hyar, Nero! Hyar, Horace! Hyar, Piner! Hyar, Belt! Hyar, Ponto! Hyar, Bugler! Hyar, Buck! Hyar, Zip!"

But the old iron jumped into another tree-top, so the man follered along, and he called the dogs: "Hyar, Shep! Hyar, Tray! Hyar, Bruce! Hyar, Rover! Hyar, Caesar! Hyar, Ring! Hyar, Nero! Hyar, Horace! Hyar, Pinder! Hyar, Belt! Hyar, Ponto! Hyar, Bugler! Hyar, Buck! Hyar, Zip!"

But the old iron jumped into another tree-top, so the man follered along, and he called the dogs; "Hyar, Shep! Hyar, Tray! Hyar, Bruce! Hyar, Rover! Hyar, Caesar! Hyar, Ring! Hyar, Nero! Hyar, Horace! Hyar, Pinder! Hyar, Belt! Hyar, Ponto! Hyar, Bugler! Hyar, Buck! Hyar, Zip!"

But the old iron jumped into another tree-top, so the man follered along, and he called the dogs: "Hyar, Shep! Hyar, Tray, Hyar, Bruce! Hyar, Rover! Hyar, Caesar! Hyar, Ring! Hyar, Nero! Hyar, Horace! Hyar, Pinder! Hyar, Belt! Hyar, Ponto! Hyar, Bugler! Hyar, Buck! Hyar, Zip!"

But the old iron jumped into another tree-top, so the man follered along, and he called the dogs: "Hyar, Shep! Hyar, Tray! Hyar, Bruce! Hyar, Rover! Hyar, Caesar! Hyar, Ring! Hyar, Nero! Hyar, Horace! Hyar, Pinder! Hyar, Belt! Hyar, Ponto! Hyar, Bugler! Hyar, Buck! Hyar, Zip!"

But the old iron jumped into another tree-top, so the man follered along, and he called the dogs . . .

Vance Randolph

The Great Riding

As a writer, I am approaching an unknown term.
Only a man should write about such an adventurer
as Hernando de Soto, that Captain of adventurers!
How can my fantasy cope with the dark bronze pieces and the stormy
gold of that wild and glittering age?
More than four centuries ago,
Don Hernando de Soto,
riding in armor between the Arkansas bayous,
you passed by my home in the Present of my Nonexistence.
If I had been here when you came– but now it is late
for the courtesy of hospitality!
You are a phantom.
Your secrets are sealed forever:
you have nothing to tell me
of that lost and haunted journey between these bayous.
The summer sun swings high and the winter sun low,
but all else you looked on is changed beyond recognition.
The swamps and ridges are fields of cotton and soybeans:
the tractors roar in the furrows:
the planes dip over:
the wild goose lands are a tangle of power lines
and flood gates and levees:
the wild duck ponds are marked.
But the air that you breathed is mine, and your Present tense
is a part of my life in the Present of my existence.

Accept then, Don Hernando, this frail medallion,
slight though it be, wrought from the bronze of the Past, set in the
stone Zero that is the Present!

Lily Peter

Alley

Dark in, just dark--
probe through apple,

a whisper with red,
with dog,

with no thing. walk
a hundred, none more

see, C the dark
apple hammer out

the miles, stuck like
"I think I can, I..."

rhymes that tick like
ants on soft pedals.

slow, cause we don't
stop, slow. in

a morse of pimples
talk

a face, a slurry
suspending a body.

and some thing flutters
like a lamp-post

placeless and happy
outside.

Pat Phillips

Biographies

Shirley Abbott

Shirley Abbott: born in 1934 in Hot Springs, a town as hustling in those days as Henry Dumas's Sweet Home, 1934, was hushed. Like the intense Henry, she would not forget much. Her father was a bookmaker, which was white-collar work in Hot Springs, the state's largest resort, and its only track town. Her mother was a homemaker and physical therapy assistant. Her family lived at 122 Alamo Street (now the site of the Royale Vista Hotel) with her father's parents and her father's younger brother and his wife. Abbott is married to Alexander Tomkievicz, a commercial artist. They have two daughters, Katharine and Elizabeth. Abbott is an editor at Rebus, Inc., in New York City.

Shirley Abbott began her literary career at *Horizon*, tutored by Joseph J. Thorndike Jr., the magazine's original editor. Neither minor physical detail nor deeply submerged analysis has escaped the orderly strata of her memory. The story of Hot Springs flows clearly through her writing as her family forms their own ring. Abbott subscribes to the *analyiste* approach to history; that is, "from the ground up." The wit and acuity of a natural intellect, the irreverence of an upstart mountaineer and an urban feminist, render her companion memoirs, *Womenfolks* and *The Bookmaker's Daughter* (a *New York Times* Notable Book of the Year for 1991), developmentally required reading.

The Bookmaker's Daughter: A Memory Unbound (Ticknor and Fields, 1991)
Historic Charleston (Knapp Press, 1985)
Womenfolks: Growing Up Down South (Ticknor and Fields, 1983)
The National Museum of American History (Abrams, 1981)
The Art of Food (Oxmoor, 1977)

Maya Angelou

Maya Angelou: born in 1928 in St. Louis, daughter of Bailey and Vivian Baxter Johnson. She spent her childhood moving back and forth between her grandmother in Stamps, Arkansas, and her mother in St. Louis. She has one son, Guy.

Maya Angelou has transformed the grievous injuries inflicted upon a child by divided and absent parents, racial discrimination, and sexual abuse into an illustrious career of cultural work. The earliest burdens were succeeded by teen years of unwanted pregnancy, menial toil, and prostitution. All of it, she changed—into an adult cosmos of autobiography, poetry, and theater. The most debilitating of these adversities could very well be the criminally insane, legally sanctioned institution of segregation; the most triumphant response has been Angelou's articulation of it in print. *I Know Why the Caged Bird Sings*, titled after a Paul Laurence Dunbar poem, marks the beginning of her literary metamorphosis. To date, five volumes comprise her autobiography. Sacred texts, Shakespeare, and the vernacular of the rural South have shaped the core of her language field. The distaff line of the family provided her with the necessary perseverance and resilience for an expressive calling. In January of 1993 she delivered the inaugural poem, "On the Pulse of Morning," for President William Jefferson Clinton. Maya Angelou is Reynolds Professor of American Studies at Wake Forest University.

I Shall Not Be Moved (Random House, 1990)

Now Sheba Sings Her Song (Dutton, 1987)

Poems (Bantam, 1987)

All God's Children Need Traveling Shoes (Random House, 1986)

The Heart of a Woman (Random House, 1981)

Singin' and Swingin' and Gettin' Merry like Christmas (Random House, 1976)

And Still I Rise (Random House, 1976)

Gather Together in My Name (Random House, 1974)

I Know Why the Caged Bird Sings (Random House, 1969)

Margaret Jones Bolsterli

Margaret Jones Bolsterli: born in Watson in 1931. Educated at the University of Arkansas, Washington University, and the University of Minnesota, she joined the faculty at the University of Arkansas in 1968. She has two sons.

Bolsterli's first book, *The Early Community at Bedford Park: "Corporate Happiness" in the First Garden Suburb,* was published by Ohio University Press in 1977. In the 1980s, as an adjunct of her research, she began editing nineteenth-century diaries. Two of these documents, along with her own memoir, have done much to enrich the record of the south-central and southeastern parts of the state, Desha County in particular, where the confluence of the White and the Arkansas and of the Arkansas and the Mississippi rivers has made the soil so rich and settlement so unstable. The 1890 diary of a farm woman, and Bolsterli's own account of a Desha County childhood in the 1930s, make for a remarkable personal, historical reading. This is black bottom land, where the soil is called gumbo and buckshot. It is a land of swamps and high water—where county seats have been swept away by flooding, generations have been decreased by fever, and where railroads went bankrupt making repairs. Bolsterli's unerring sentences convey a mental strengthening; they compel a lucidity. As the woods around Watson closed in on its inhabitants, the wordsmiths therein learned to illumine their private space.

A Remembrance of Eden: Harriet Bailey Bullock Daniels' Memories of a Frontier Plantation in Arkansas, 1849–1872, edited with an introduction by Margaret J. Bolsterli (University of Arkansas Press, 1993)

Born in the Delta: Reflections on the Making of a Southern White Sensibility (University of Tennessee Press, 1991)

Vinegar Pie and Chicken Bread: A Woman's Diary of Life in the Rural South, 1890–1891, edited with an introduction by Margaret J. Bolsterli (University of Arkansas Press, 1983)

Besmilr Brigham

Besmilr Brigham: born 1913, Pace, Mississippi, with Choctaw predecessors on both sides. Educated at Mary Hardin-Baylor College in Texas and the New School for Social Research in New York City. Besmilr Brigham lives in Horatio with Roy, her husband of nearly sixty years. They have one daughter, Heloise.

Besmilr Brigham's most energetic publishing years spanned only seven years, from 1969 to 1976, but over the past fifty years she has completed several dozen manuscripts, of both prose and poetry. The titles alone testify to her auto-didacticism and originality: *The Firebird Heart, Blue Fields of Maljnche, A Light in the Water, To Live as a Bird, Death and the Negrito, Loco el Santo, Dark Field, Decoy of the Wild Duck, The Janus Ring, Yaki, The Storm, Poems for the Lago, Year of the False Spring,* and more. While her literary friendships and acquaintances have included John Gould Fletcher, Robert Creeley, Robert Duncan, and her son-in-law, poet Keith Wilson, Brigham is best appreciated as a loner. She and her husband have been nomadic to say the least, camping out for months at a time, in Mexico, Central America, France, and Canada. They have lived in major cities and on both coasts of the United States. The tiny town of Horatio, Arkansas, could not be a more unlikely place to find a writer who received a 1970 Discovery Award from the National Endowment for the Arts in the company of Raymond Carver, Alice Walker, Lucille Clifton, Louise Gluck, Fanny Howe, Simon Ortiz, Hugh Seidman, and others. She published in such salient magazines as *The Atlantic Monthly* and *Harper's Bazaar.* She anthologized poems and stories with New Directions, Houghton Mifflin, Random House, and Simon and Schuster, and in 1971 she brought out a book with Knopf. But, off and on, for thirty years, Horatio has been home to the writer, her husband, and her cats. Cats she has—balled up, draped, and sprawling throughout her definitively Arkansas house. Brigham is a rarely-troved-or-honored-these-days poet-of-the-physical-world, her three acres of which are situated in the blistering southwest corner of Arkansas. She knows its snakes, birds, and trees, and they are as responsive to her as she to them. To come upon her and her work in all of its intense regard, its uniquely regulated breath, and its artistic fullness was an unforeseen gift of this pilgrimage.

Heaved from the Earth (Knopf, 1971)
Agony Dance: Death of the Dancing Dolls (Winepress Publishing, 1969)
The Thirteenth Mask: Games for an Easter Child, the script for a dance/lyric
      drama, produced at Mythic Theatre, Phoenix, Arizona. Date not given.

Dee Alexander Brown

Dee Alexander Brown: born in 1908 in Alberta, Louisiana; grew up in Stephens (Ouachita County). He lives in Little Rock with Sally (Sara Baird Stroud), his wife of over fifty years. They have two children, Mitchell and Linda.

He worked first as a linotype operator, then as a rookie reporter for the *Harrison Times,* arriving in the late 1920s on the Missouri and North Arkansas line known locally as May Never Arrive. He was hired as a library assistant in the college library in Conway, and later as a low-ranking civil servant at the Agriculture Library in Washington, then as technical librarian for the Technical Information Branch Library at the U.S. Army's Aberdeen Proving Ground in Maryland. He joined the staff of the Agriculture Library at the University of Illinois beginning in 1948. From 1962 to 1975 he held the rank of professor at Illinois. Brown always knew how to situate himself among books. In the thirties he won third prize in a short-story contest. His first novel satirized political life in Washington. It was suppressed on the eve of publication because of the war, and "a patriotic book" was commissioned in its stead. Brown has written consistently for hire and for pleasure. His skills as both a trained and self-styled researcher, and as a voluntary word slave, integrated perfectly when he wrote *Bury My Heart at Wounded Knee*. In the process of writing *Wounded Knee,* he adopted an emboldening mantra: "I am a very, very old Indian, and I'm remembering the past. And I'm looking toward the Atlantic Ocean . . . I kept that viewpoint every night. That's all I did." The vast subject that elected him, paired with his characteristic empathy, concentrated upon this nocturnal composition to create an American classic.

Brown is one of the most widely read and most honored of contemporary writers of the American West. He is the author of twenty-seven books of fiction and nonfiction.

When the Century Was Young: A Writer's Notebook (August House, 1993)
Wondrous Times on the Frontier (August House, 1991, hardcover; Harper Perennial, 1991, paper)
Conspiracy of Knaves (Henry Holt, 1986)
Killdeer Mountain (Henry Holt, 1983)
Creek Mary's Blood (Henry Holt, 1980)
Hear That Lonesome Whistle Blow (Henry Holt, 1977; Chattto and Windus, 1977)
Bury My Heart at Wounded Knee: An Indian History of the American West (Henry Holt, 1970; First Owl Book Edition, 1991)
The Gentle Tamers: Women of the Old Wild West (Putnam, 1958; University of Nebraska Press, 1968, 1981, a Bison Book)

Andrea Hollander Budy

Andrea Hollander Budy: born in Berlin in 1947. After schooling in Boston and teaching in the West, she came with her husband, Todd, to settle in the Arkansas Ozarks. They have a son, Brooke. They run the Wildflower Bed and Breakfast in Mountain View.

Informed by personal experience and independent reading or what is known as being "apprenticed to the page," Budy's poetry is tooled around a fairly remote, contemplative life lived in the woods of her own mind's Stone County. A more private life goes on inside, in spite of the innkeeper's very socially occupied public life. Landscape may compete with society for attention, but in the poetry, the result is an engaging level of tension. Her poems have earned her the Arkansas Porter Fund Award (founded by Arkansas writers Sid McMath and Jack Butler), the Nicholas Roerich Poetry Prize, and a fellowship from the National Endowment for the Arts. By the end of the eighties her work had begun to appear in several literary magazines, including *Poetry, The Ohio Review, Zone,* and *The Georgia Review.*

House without a Dreamer (Story Line Press, 1993)

Chapbooks:

What the Other Eye Sees (Wayland Press, 1991)
Happily Ever After (Panhandler Press of the University of West Florida, 1989)
Living on the Cusp (Moonsquilt Press, 1981)

Jack Butler

Jack Butler: born in Alligator, Mississippi, in 1944. He is the son of a Baptist preacher and a homemaker. He was educated at Central Missouri State College, where he concentrated in English and mathematics, and at the University of Arkansas, where he earned an M.F.A. in writing. He has two children from his first marriage, Lynnika and Sarah, and two stepchildren from his marriage to Jayme Thomas Tull, Sherri and Catherine. For a number of years, Butler made a living as an actuarial analyst for Blue Cross/Blue Shield and as a consultant in the same field. He recently left a deanship at Hendrix College in Conway to teach at Santa Fe College in New Mexico.

Butler is a poet, short-story writer, and novelist. He is also a cognoscente and a writer of science fiction (*Nightshade*). He has been quoted as saying his fiction travels from the Mississippi Delta to the stars, which makes the work resistant to category. He is comfortable crossing the cosmic with the comic, and his most recent novel is lit up by both. It is narrated by the Holy Ghost and set in the state's capitol at the time of the latest creation-science trial, in 1981. Like his friend, novelist Donald Harington, Butler is proficient with dialect so that a certain athleticism is required to keep pace with his prose. A *Washington Post* reviewer wrote of *Living in Little Rock with Miss Little Rock,* "If you have the patience of a saint, a weakness for wordplay and a love of the language, this remarkable performance is not to be missed."

Living in Little Rock with Miss Little Rock (Knopf, 1993)
Nightshade (Atlantic Monthly Press, 1989)
Jujitsu for Christ (August House, 1986; Penguin, 1988)
The Kid Who Wanted to Be a Spaceman: Poems (August House, 1984)
Hawk Gumbo and Other Stories (August House, 1983)
West of Hollywood: Poems from a Hermitage (August House, 1980)

Crescent Dragonwagon

Crescent Dragonwagon: born in 1952 in New York City. She grew up in Hastings-on-Hudson, a suburb of the city. Crescent, who was originally named Ellen Zolotow, is the daughter of writers Charlotte Zolotow and Maurice Zolotow. She has a brother, Stephen. Crescent moved to Eureka Springs, Arkansas, in 1972. She is married to Ned Shanks. They are the innkeepers of Dairy Hollow House, a country inn and restaurant in Eureka Springs, where Crescent is also head chef.

Crescent Dragonwagon began writing books for her kingdom of dolls as a little girl. She became a professional writer at nineteen with the publication of her first children's book, *Rainy Day Together* (Harper, 1970), and her first cookbook, *The Commune Cookbook* (Simon and Schuster, 1971), a short three years after she dropped out of school. She has since published several dozen children's books, young adult novels, novels, poetry collections, and cookbooks. To say, "I just finished reading your new cookbook," is as appropriate a response to a Dragonwagon cookbook as to say, "I use that book all the time." She writes and she cooks; she cooks and she writes, and she has a thorough understanding of her ingredients. Her love of Eureka Springs is distributed throughout the articles, the books for children (*The Itch Book, Katie in the Morning, Home Place*), and the two Dairy Hollow House cookbooks.

Dairy Hollow House Soup and Bread: A Country Inn Cookbook (Workman
    Publishing Company, 1992)
Annie Flies the Birthday Bike (Macmillan, 1992)
Alligators and Others, All Year Long, illustrated by Aruego (Macmillan, 1992)
Winter Holding Spring, illustrated by Himler (Macmillan, 1990)
The Itch Book, illustrated by Joseph Mahler (Macmillan, 1990)
Home Place, illustrated by Pinkney (Macmillan, 1990)
This Is the Bread I Baked for Ned, illustrated by Isadore Seltzer (Macmillan,
    1989)
Margaret Ziegler Is Horse Crazy, illustrated by Peter Elwell (Macmillan, 1988)
Dear Miss Moshki, illustrated by Diane Palmisciano (Macmillan, 1988)
Diana, Maybe, illustrated by Deborah Kogan Ray (Macmillan, 1987)
Half a Moon and One Whole Star, illustrated by Jerry Pinkney (Macmillan,
    1986)
The Dairy Hollow House Cookbook, with Jan Brown, illustrated by Jacqueline
    Froelich (Macmillan, 1986)
The Year It Rained (Macmillan, 1985)

Henry Dumas

Henry Dumas: born in 1934 in Sweet Home; died in 1968, two months shy of
his thirty-fourth birthday, in the New York subway system at the hand of a tran-
sit policeman. Dumas attended City College and Rutgers University. He spent
four years in the air force. He was married to Loretta Ponton; they had two sons,
David and Michael.

Remembrances of Henry Dumas by writer friends and next-of-kin are
unanimous with regard to his physical energy, his mental intensity, and his spir-
itual magnanimity. Dumas's confidence translated into eloquence, his inspira-
tion into actual achievement. Though Henry Dumas was shattered by banal
force, the writing remains vital. He is a southern writer and a northern writer,
a natural writer and an artificer. He is a realist and a surrealist. He wrote with

rage and love. He was knife-sharp. Reviewers have linked his literary influences to Jean Toomer, Langston Hughes, and Zora Neale Hurston. They have noted his own influence upon Alice Walker, Toni Morrison, and Paule Marshall. Dumas was thoroughly conscious of and at home in his culture, rural and urban: gospel, blues, religion, poetry, folk arts, jazz. In addition to publishing his own poems and stories, Dumas was vigorously involved in developing and editing literary magazines such as *Umbra, Camel, American Weave, Hiram Poetry Review,* and *Negro Digest.* His books were published posthumously; thanks to his literary executor, poet Eugene B. Redmond, the books comprise an organic whole. In a sense, the work of Henry Dumas was the seed for this statewide project. Visiting his hometown, reading his poems and stories, I was repeatedly struck by the quality of his art and by the impact it was having elsewhere. I felt that the community center, the school, whatever was public, useful, and remotely promising in his hometown should bear his name, because what he produced is primary—our culture—and neglecting it threatens the prospects of other potential contributors to a sane, literate society. Blaze this tree: Henry was here. "He ain't all dead either."★

Knees of a Natural Man: The Selected Poetry of Henry Dumas, edited with an
    introduction by Eugene B. Redmond (Thunder's Mouth Press, 1989)
Goodbye, Sweetwater: New and Selected Stories, edited with an introduction by
    Eugene B. Redmond (Thunder's Mouth Press, 1988)
Rope of Wind and Other Stories, edited with an introduction by Eugene B.
    Redmond (Random House, 1979)
Jonoah and the Green Stone (1976)
Play Ebony, Play Ivory (1974)
Ark of Bones and Other Stories (1974)

★from "Echo Tree"

Donald Harington

Donald Harington: born in 1935 in Little Rock. He has three daughters from his first marriage: Jennifer, Calico, and Katy. He now lives in Fayetteville with his wife, Kim, and teaches art history at the University of Arkansas.

Throughout his childhood, he summered in the Ozark hamlet of Drakes Creek. He has graduate degrees in art from Boston University and from the University of Arkansas, to which—after years of teaching at Wyndham College in Vermont—he has returned. With his 1970 novel, *Lightning Bug*, Harington introduced the invented hamlet of Stay More, the capital seat of his imagination. But from the opening sentence of the first novel, *The Cherry Pit*, Arkansas hill country would be his Yoknapatawpha County. He is an idiosyncratic writer, which means his work is not readily classified or assimilated. Deafened in childhood, Harington's ear for hill speech is nonetheless hard to refute. Everywhere in his writing, one evidences an unusual combination of talents. The language is lyric; the humor is broad and unremitting. The story line convinces, however improbable. His action is, more often than not, picaresque. Each novel and work of nonfiction sustains the material in an original form. Structurally, Harington is not simply adept—if the novel requires poetry, the character fabricates an entire collection of poems (*Some Other Place. The Right Place,* 1972). More than one reviewer has tied him to Nabokov. His 1975 novel *The Architecture of the Arkansas Ozarks* is forever nailed to the big oak in its readers' minds.

Ekatrina (Harcourt Brace Jovanovich, 1993)

The Cockroaches of Stay More (Harcourt Brace Jovanovich, 1989)

Let Us Build Us a City: Eleven Lost Towns, nonfiction (Harcourt Brace Jovanovich, 1986)

The Architecture of the Arkansas Ozarks (Harcourt Brace Jovanovich, 1975)

Some Other Place. The Right Place. (Harcourt Brace Jovanovich, 1972)

Lightning Bug (Harcourt Brace Jovanovich, 1970)

The Cherry Pit (Harcourt Brace Jovanovich, 1965)

Jo McDougall

Jo McDougall: born in 1935 in Little Rock. Her husband, Charles McDougall, a former rice farmer, is now a commercial real-estate appraiser in Kansas City. They have two children, Charla and Duke, both of whom farm in Arkansas.

McDougall's father's parents came from Belgium to Louisiana and began to raise rice there before moving to Arkansas. She grew up on a rice farm in DeWitt. She remembers her mother reading the entire My Book House series to her. Young Jo read Shakespeare, the Bible, Yeats, Dickinson . . . She and Charles leased out their farm in Stuttgart in 1979; they lost it in the eighties along with thousands of other Delta families. The poet received her M.F.A. in 1985 from the University of Arkansas, where she studied with Miller Williams and James Whitehead. Jo McDougall teaches English and creative writing at Pittsburg State University in Kansas. She writes a lean, stoic line; each poem makes its mark, like spit.

Towns Facing Railroads (University of Arkansas Press, 1991), a collection of
    poems, which was also produced as a theater piece at Pittsburg State
    University, May 1993
The Woman in the Next Booth (Book Mark Press, 1987)

Chapbooks:

Women Who Marry Houses (Coyote Love Press, 1983)
The New Look Trio (South and West, 1965)
A Lemon Yeast and Other Mornings (South and West, 1964)

Robert Palmer: born in Little Rock in 1945. He is the son of Robert Franklin and Marguerite (Bowers) Palmer. He received a B.A. in 1967 from the University of Arkansas at Little Rock. He currently lives in New Orleans and is at work on a television series for BBC on the history of rock and roll.

As a musician, music critic, and music producer, Palmer is one of the great articulators of down-home blues, a medium he insists "needs no interpreters or popularizers." Palmer's music criticism is invariably praised for the accuracy and breadth of his research, and just as enthusiastically, for the pure pleasure the writing delivers. The involvement of his talents are total, and the talents themselves considerable. Palmer has played blues, rock, soul, and jazz on both the saxophone and the clarinet. He was a member of Insect Trust in the late sixties, and played with The Seam and Panther Burns in the eighties and nineties. He has recorded with Ornette Coleman and Bono and with Keith Richards and Ron Wood on the anti-apartheid album *Sun City*. He produces music, and he has both the instinct and the expertise to ferret out the best: his latest productions are recordings by Junior Kimbrough and the Soul Blues Boys and by CeDell Davis (both on Fat Possum Records). He writes lyrics, liner notes, articles, and books that convey a powerful connection to and a comprehensive understanding of the art and science of the blues, not to mention its progeny, rock and roll. Palmer's documentary film work includes writing and codirecting *The World According to John Coltrane* and writing and directing the music for *Deep Blues: A Tour of Mississippi Juke Joints* based on his award-winning book by the same title.

The Rolling Stones (Doubleday, 1983)

Jerry Lee Lewis Rocks! (Delilah, 1981)

Deep Blues (Viking, 1981)

A Tale of Two Cities: Memphis Rock and New Orleans Roll (Institute for Studies in American Music, Brooklyn College of the City University of New York, 1979)

Baby, That Was Rock and Roll: The Legendary Leiber and Stoller, with an introduction by John Hahr (Harcourt Brace Jovanovich, 1978)

Lily Peter

Lily Peter: born in 1891, Big Cypress Bayou (Monroe County); died in 1991 in Marvell.

One of five children of William Oliver Peter and Florence Mobrey, Miss Peter was an educator, an amateur photographer, a philanthropist, a composer, musician, and poet. Former governor Dale Bumpers named her poet laureate of Arkansas; in 1970 the *Arkansas Democrat* named her Woman of the Year. Miss Lily, as she was called, brought Van Cliburn to Helena (along with the Phillips County Community Center in which he performed) and Eugene Ormandy and the Philadelphia Orchestra to Little Rock: "Presented to the music lovers of Arkansas and the surrounding states as a gift from Miss Lily Peter." She raised a turquoise-housed cotton gin and reduced the use of pesticides in Marvell. She also brought a rescued owl, King Solomon, no less, to the 14th Annual Grand Prairie Festival of Arts. Peter was educated at Memphis State University and Vanderbilt. During World War II she taught in the high schools of Helena and Marvell, where, by her account, she was pressed to teach every subject in the curriculum except shorthand and physical education. From 1948 until her death, she owned and operated two 4,000-acre cotton farms, Ratio Plantation and Peter Plantation in Phillips and Monroe counties, along with a gin south of Marvell.

The Great Riding (1966; University of Arkansas Press, reprint, 1983)
In the Beginning: Myths of the Western World, retold in poetry and prose
    (University of Arkansas Press, 1983)
The Sea Dream of the Mississippi (1973)
The Green Linen of Summer (Robert Moore Allen, 1964)

Pat Phillips: born in 1958 in Blytheville, the son of a second-generation Ford dealer, farmer, and entrepreneur. His grandfather was the son of a farm boss for Wilson Farms, one of the state's largest. His maternal grandmother taught English and Latin at North Little Rock High. Both of his mother's parents taught at A&M in Monticello. His great-grandfather was the principal and "professor" at Valley Springs Academy in Boone County, the "Athens of Arkansas," from 1890 to 1900. His mother was an actor, attending the Yale Graduate School on a scholarship in dramatic arts. She works for the American Cancer Society in Little Rock. His uncle is the columnist Charles Albright, "The Arkansas Traveler." His father monitors the health and safety of bridge workers for the city of New York. Pat Phillips has been a union printer and a low-paid stringer for Pacifica and Monitor Radio in the States and in the Philippines. He has gutted buildings and remodeled interiors for a living. He has been a computer jockey and troubleshooter in New York City. He is presently a graduate student at Brown University and lives in Providence with his wife, painter Laura Sue King.

Phillips studied with Thom Gunn and Michael Palmer at the University of California, Berkeley. He credits Palmer's influence on his understanding of "the word as a construct of the world." In fact, the word is the unit upon which he concentrates; the whole is subsumed by its value or, as he might say, its moment. Pat Phillips's language is deviant and recondite. It is spare and physical. The poems will not stay put. His poems and critical essays have appeared in several literary magazines.

"Day as Sargasso: A Reading of Jean Day's *The I and the You*" (*Object*, 1993)
"Twos," seven poems from *N* (*Impercipient*, 1993)
"Marriage" (*The Berkeley Poetry Review*, 1990)
"O" (*Prism*, 1990)
"Alley" (*Sulfur*, 1989)
"Child" (*Sulfur*, 1989)
"Features" (*Sulfur*, 1989)

Vance Randolph

Vance Randolph: born in 1892 in Pittsburg, Kansas; died in 1980 in Fayetteville. Randolph was introduced to the Ozarks on a family vacation in 1899. Beginning in 1947, he made the hills his permanent residence. He spent his adult life collecting and preserving, annotating and interpreting traditional life of the Ozark Mountains. He would eventually be recognized as the far-sighted pioneer he was. While Randolph completed his graduate work in psychology at Clark University and undertook postgraduate work at the University of Kansas, he was, in bone and spirit, a maverick. As a hack/ghost writer he was versatile in the extreme; his pseudonyms waxed expert on fields as incompatible as etiquette and prostitution. Whether Randolph is dubbed a collector or elevated to folklorist, he was both an original and prodigious compiler/writer. As a fiction writer he limited himself to one collection of tales *From an Ozark Holler* (1933), one juvenile book, *The Camp on Wildcat Creek* (Knopf, 1934), and one novel, *Hedwig* (1935). The art of fiction would be for Randolph a foray not a forte. Literally thousands of regional songs, tales, superstitions, remedies, anecdotes, jokes, et cetera, would be reclaimed due to his avidity for the whole story lore of the hills. His first decade of research culminated in *The Ozarks: An American Survival of Primitive Society* (1931). The last major collections to appear during his lifetime were *Ozark Folklore: A Bibliography* (1972) and *Pissing in the Snow* (1976). An honorary Ph.D. was awarded him from the University of Arkansas in 1951, and June 12, 1976, was proclaimed Vance Randolph Day throughout the state of Arkansas; yet he would be fully eighty-six before being elected a Fellow of the American Folklore Society, the one accolade that mattered to him. Forever the dissenting, noninstitutional man, Vance Randolph provided a specific place with a description which would have otherwise been smoothed over by strip malls and pimpled with satellite dishes, leaving only a mean record of having ever been distinct.

Blow the Candle Out: "Unprintable" Ozark Folksongs and Folklore, Vol. 2, Folk Rhymes and Other Lore, edited with an introduction by G. Legman (University of Arkansas Press, 1992)

Roll Me in Your Arms: "Unprintable" Ozark Folksongs and Folklore, Vol. 1, Folksongs and Music, edited with an introduction by G. Legman (University of Arkansas Press, 1992)

Pissing in the Snow and Other Ozark Folktales (University of Illinois Press, 1976; Avon Books, 1977)

Ozark Folklore: A Bibliography (Indiana University Press, 1972)

Hot Springs and Hell, and Other Folk Jests and Anecdotes from the Ozarks (Folklore Associates, 1965)

Sticks in the Knapsack and Other Ozark Folktales (Columbia University Press, 1958)

The Talking Turtle and Other Ozark Folktales (Columbia University Press, 1957)

The Devil's Pretty Daughter and Other Ozark Folktales (Columbia University Press, 1955)

Down in the Holler: A Gallery of Ozark Folk Speech (University of Oklahoma Press, 1953); reprinted as *Stiff as a Poker* (Barnes and Noble, 1993)

Who Blowed Up the Church House? and Other Ozark Folk Tales (Columbia University Press, 1952)

We Always Lie to Strangers (Columbia University Press, 1951)

Ozark Folksongs (1946–1950, four vols., State Historical Society of Missouri)

Ozark Superstitions (Columbia University Press, 1947); reprinted as *Ozark Magic and Folklore* (Dover, 1964)

An Ozark Anthology (American Caxton Society Press, 1940)

Hedwig (Vanguard, 1935)

Ozark Mountain Folks (Vanguard, 1932)

The Ozarks: An American Survival of Primitive Society (Vanguard, 1931)

Frank "Son" Seals

Frank "Son" Seals: born in Osceola in 1942. His father, Jim "Son" Seals, played the trombone and performed with F. S. Wolcott's Rabbit Foot Minstrels. Jim Seals also owned the Dipsy Doodle Club in Osceola, which exposed his "Son" to the deep blues gods when he was very young.

By the time Seals was thirteen, he had already played drums for Robert Nighthawk. In the early sixties, he toured with Earl Hooker's Road Masters and soon after with Albert King. He could often be heard with his own band at the Chez Paris in Little Rock and The Blue Goose and the Harlem Club in Osceola before he moved to Chicago in 1971. While he continues to tour on weekends, he performs three nights a week at Queen Bee's on Chicago's South Side. Seals started on the drums, but he has made his mark with guitar, vocals, and lyrics. Even his laugh is a signature. Since the 1976 Alligator release of *Midnight Son,* Seals' status in the blues annals has been assured. He has been a houserocker for nearly forty years and is not backing down. *The Chicago Reader* named him the Best Chicago Blues Artist of the Year in 1974; the Downbeat International Critics Award in Soul and Rhythm and Blues went to Seals as the best under-recognized artist in 1977, and in 1984 W. C. Handy Blues Awards chose *Bad Axe* as the Contemporary Blues Album of the Year.

In addition to his burning performances, Seals has often been cited for his stinging, original lyrics. Among the recordings written by Son Seals are the following:

"Don't Bother Me"
"Don't Fool with My Baby"
"Four Full Seasons of Love"
"Going Back Home"
"Hot Sauce"
"Your Love Is Like a Cancer"
"Woman in Black"
"Arkansas Woman"
"Bad Axe"
"My Life"

These sides and other originals appear on *Midnight Son* (1976), *Bad Axe* (1984), *Living in the Danger Zone* (1991), and *Live and Burning* (1992), all produced by Eyeball Music, Alligator Records and Artist Management, Inc.

Frank Stanford

Frank Stanford: born in 1948 in southeast Mississippi. In Frank Stanford's twenty-nine years (he died in Fayetteville in 1978), he published nine collections of poetry, including a 542-page opus, *The Battlefield Where the Moon Says I Love You.* He was the adopted son of Dorothy Gilbert, at that time Firestone's only female manager, and of Albert Franklin Stanford, a levee contractor. Stanford's family left the Tennessee delta for the Arkansas Ozarks when he was still a child. He attended high school at the Benedictine Monastery and Academy in Subiaco, Arkansas. He attended the University of Arkansas off and on, but left without taking a degree. He married twice. His second marriage was to painter Ginny Crouch. Stanford earned his living as a land surveyor. He was founding editor of Lost Roads Publishers, a book press which issued twelve titles under his direction, and which continues to operate under the joint editorship of Forrest Gander and C. D. Wright.

Frank Stanford both read and wrote prodigiously; evidently he did so at all times, under every condition. There are poems in his published collections dating from 1957, when he was preposterously only nine years old. The work is that continuous. In addition to the books, his legacy entails several dozen manuscripts in various states of completion: poems, translations, stories, interviews, essays, and film scripts. At his best, Stanford was an abundant poet, both in word and scope. Once the poet had achieved fluency, which he did at a very early age, there boomed the weight of what he had to say, the matter of urgency. Finally, there is the work.

The Light the Dead See: The Selected Poems of Frank Stanford, edited with an
    introduction by Leon Stokesbury (University of Arkansas Press, 1991)

Conditions Uncertain and Likely to Pass Away: Tales by Frank Stanford (Lost
     Roads Publishers, 1989)
You (Lost Roads Publishers, 1979)
Crib Death (Ironwood Press, 1978)
The Battlefield Where the Moon Says I Love You (Lost Roads Publishers with
     Mill Mountain Press, 1977)
The Singing Knives (Mill Mountain Press, 1972; Lost Roads Publishers, 1979)

Chapbooks:
Constant Stranger (Mill Mountain Press, 1976)
Arkansas Bench Stone (Mill Mountain Press, 1975)
Field Talk (Mill Mountain Press, 1975)
Shade (Mill Mountain Press, 1975)
Ladies from Hell (Mill Mountain Press, 1974)

James Whitehead

James Whitehead: born in St. Louis in 1936. He married Gen Graeber from
Yazoo City; they have seven children.

Whitehead's great-great-grandfather, Addison MacArthur Bourland, was an
Arkansas surgeon, linguist, and writer. Bourland earned his medical degree at
the University of Nashville, soon to be Vanderbilt. Whitehead was educated at
Vanderbilt (B.A. in philosophy, M.A. in English) and the University of Iowa
(M.F.A. in poetry and fiction). In high school he played football and thought
about "making a preacher." Soon after going to Vanderbilt he wrote his last ser-
mon in blank verse. Whitehead is strongly identified both with Mississippi,
where he grew up and taught for a time at Millsaps College, and Arkansas, where
he cofounded the creative writing program at the University of Arkansas in
Fayetteville. Reviewing *Joiner* in the *The New York Times Book Review,* R. V.
Cassill wrote of the novel: "What Whitehead has achieved is to sound the full
range of the Deep South's exultation and lamentation. His tirade makes an awesome, fearful and glorious impact on the mind and ear."

Near at Hand (University of Missouri Press, 1993)
Local Men (University of Illinois Press, 1979)
Joiner (Knopf, 1971; University of Arkansas Press, reprint, 1991)
Domains (Louisiana State University Press, 1966)

Chapbook:

Actual Size (Trilobite Press, 1985)

Miller Williams

Miller Williams: born in Hoxie in 1930, son of a Methodist preacher who was active in efforts to establish the Southern Tenant Farmers' Union. Williams has three children from his first marriage: Lucinda, Robert, and Karyn. He lives with his wife, Jordan, in Fayetteville.

Holding degrees in zoology, Williams taught college chemistry and biology before deferring to poetry. Despite or because of his religious and scientific background, he insists that his "priorities are horizontal, not vertical." Williams says, "I question the objectively comprehensible universe . . . but at the same time I write in a narrative framework filled with the furniture of this world . . . What gets called into question is not the world itself but our ideas about it, our orderings of it." Miller Williams has been on the faculty of the English Department at the University of Arkansas since 1971 and has held the rank of University Professor since 1987. Prior to returning to Arkansas, he taught at Louisiana State University, Loyola University (where he founded the *New Orleans Review*), University of Chile (where he began translating Nicanor Parra), and the National University of Mexico. In addition to his poetry and translations, he has published books on a variety of subjects, including critical books on John Crowe Ransom and John Ciardi. His awards include the Amy Lowell Award in Poetry, the Prix de Rome for Literature, and the Poets' Prize. Miller Williams is founding director of the University of Arkansas Press.

Adjusting to the Light: Poems (University of Missouri Press, 1992)

Living on the Surface: *New and Selected Poems* (Louisiana State University Press, 1989)

Imperfect Love (Louisiana State University Press, 1986)

The Boys on Their Bony Mules (Louisiana State University Press, 1986)

Distractions (Louisiana State University Press, 1981)

Sonnets of Giuseppe Belli (Louisiana State University Press, 1981)

Why God Permits Evil (Louisiana State University Press, 1977)

Halfway from Hoxie: *New and Selected Poems* (E. P. Dutton, 1973)

Emergency Poems: *Nicanor Parra* (New Directions, 1972)

Sonny Boy Williamson

Sonny Boy Williamson aka Footsie, The Goat, Little Boy Blue, Rice Miller, and christened Aleck or Alex, son of Millie Ford and stepfather Jim Miller. Generally believed: born in 1897, though dates of 1884, 1899, and 1909 have been given (he said of himself he was an "1800 man"), in Tallahatchie County, Mississippi. In 1948 he wed Mattie Jones. Williamson died in 1965 in Helena. Sonny Boy Williamson came to musical maturity in Helena, Arkansas, where the Sonny Boy Blues Society was founded in 1988, honoring the harmonica player's name and the genre in which he was a virtuoso player and a gifted lyricist. He also performed and recorded on guitar.

Unfortunately, Sonny Boy Williamson's name was borrowed from a contemporary, also a mouth harpist, already well established in Chicago. If Sonny Boy "John Lee" Williamson made the harmonica a solo instrument, Sonny Boy "Rice Miller" made it an orchestra. The dual appellation aided and detracted from both careers. The long and dapper, difficult and enigmatic Sonny Boy "Rice Miller" Williamson performed with many other blues legends, including Tampa Red, Baby Boy Warren, Pinetop Perkins, Houston Stackhouse, and Otis Spann. His longest-term partnership was with Robert Jr. Lockwood. In 1941 he and Lockwood approached Helena businessman Sam Anderson, who was starting a radio station; soon thereafter they became KFFA's King Biscuit Entertainers, reaching a wide Delta audience with their own music, the blues. Sonny Boy's recording contract with Trumpet, Lillian McMurry's label in Jackson, Mississippi, was sold eventually to Chess, the preeminent Chicago blues label. In 1951 at fifty-eight, intractable as ever, he recorded first with Muddy Water's band and re-teamed with Robert Lockwood for his second Chess session. His recording years continued, erratically, through 1965. In the early sixties, songs of Sonny Boy's would be recorded by John Mayall and Led Zeppelin. After a European tour ended in 1963, he went on to Poland with Memphis Slim, then back to England to tour with the Yardbirds and The Animals. He toured Europe again in 1964, but in the spring of 1965 he came full circle, home to Helena, to record at the KFFA studio. During his last weeks he jammed with Ronnie Hawkins's old back-up group in Helena, soon to be The Band, including, of course, the drummer from Marvell, Levon Helm. There was talk of working together, but Sonny Boy died on May 25, 1965, in his apartment over Newkirk Auto Shop, missing his studio call at KFFA for the last time. Since 1986 the King Biscuit Blues Festival, initiated by Bubba Sullivan, has brought the blues to Helena on a national scale, an ongoing tribute to its original "king biscuit." Among Sonny Boy Williamson's classic contributions to the blues are the following:

"Eyesight to the Blind" (1951)
"Mighty Long Time" (1951)
"Don't Start Me to Talkin'" (1955)
"Don't Lose Your Eye" (1955)
"Fattening Frogs for Snakes" (1957)
"Your Funeral and My Trial" (1958)
"Keep Your Hand Out of My Pocket" (1958)
"Nine Below Zero" (1961)
"Help Me" (1963)

Sonny Boy Williamson: The Chess Years (all titles composed by Williamson and published by Arc Music Corporation, 1991). This compilation has eighty-nine sides. Note: Only Chess recording dates are given, with the exception of "Mighty Long Time," which the company did not re-record.

C. Vann Woodward

C. Vann Woodward: born in 1908 in eastern Arkansas in Vanndale, which bears his family name. He spent most of his youth in Morrilton, where his father was public school superintendent. He was educated at Henderson College in Arkadelphia, Emory University, Columbia, and the University of North Carolina. He married Glenn Boyd MacLeod in 1937. They had one child, Peter.

In a career extending over half a century, C. Vann Woodward has created a fluid yet complex history of the American South. He has been skillful at making his influential learning available to the profession as well as to a more general reading audience. Woodward's scholarship is impeccably qualified, his analyses acute, and his prose as artful as the finest of our traditional novelists. His has been a continuing examination of our profoundest issues. Twenty years beyond the original publication of *Origins of the New South,* Michael O'Brien observed, "Seldom can a subject have been raised from such obscurity to such illumination at a single bound. Just as a piece of technique, an effort of research, it was a virtuoso performance." Furthermore, "he (Woodward) maintained its fresh moral geography throughout the work with a tenacity whose coherence made it one of the few works of art that Southern historical literature has produced."

Among his important edited texts is the extremely valuable "diary in fact/diary in form" of Mary Chesnut. In 1982 C. Vann Woodward was the winner of the Pulitzer Prize in history for *Mary Chesnut's Civil War* (Yale University Press, 1981).

Comer Vann Woodward is Sterling Professor of History Emeritus at Yale University. He lives outside of New Haven.

The Old World's New World (New York Public Library and Oxford
    University Press, 1992)
The Future of the Past (Oxford University Press, 1989)
Thinking Back: The Perils of Writing History (Louisiana State University Press,
    1986)

American Counterpoint: Slavery and Racism in the North-South Dialogue (Little, Brown, 1971)

The Burden of Southern History (Louisiana State University Press, 1960; revised, 1968)

The Strange Career of Jim Crow (Oxford University Press, 1955; revised with a new introduction, 1957; revised, 1966, 1974)

Origins of the New South, 1877–1913 (Louisiana State University Press, 1951; revised, 1971)

Reunion and Reaction: The Compromise of 1877 and the End of Reconstruction (Little, Brown, 1951; revised, 1966)

The Battle for Leyte Gulf (Macmillan, 1957; Landborough, 1958)

Tom Watson, Agrarian Rebel (Macmillan, 1938; reprinted with an introduction, 1958; Oxford University Press, 1963, 1975)

An Arkansas Reader's Source Key

The following is intended only as a skeleton of sources reasonably available to anyone studying Arkansas literature. Any isolated genre or subgenre such as songwriting or homilies or epistolaries would quickly direct you along a more pertinent route. Most of these are general edited texts and anthologies, which are no substitute for ample reading in individual voices, but which may help single out those upon which you wish to concentrate.

Arkansas: A Guide to the State. New York: Hastings House, 1941. Reprinted with a new introduction by Elliott West. *The WPA Guide to the 1930s Arkansas.* Lawrence: University Press of Kansas, 1987.

Arkansas in Short Fiction: Stories from 1841–1984. Edited by William M. Baker and Ethel C. Simpson. Little Rock, Ark.: August House, 1986.

Arkansas Voices. Edited by Sarah Jane Fountain. Little Rock: Rose Publishing Company, 1941. Revised edition. Conway: University of Central Arkansas, 1989. Note: I consider the first edition stronger than the revised edition.

Behold, Our Works Were Good. A Handbook of Arkansas Women's History. Edited by Elizabeth Jacoway (Arkansas Women's History Institute in association with August House, 1988).

Dillard, Tom, and Michael Dougan. *Arkansas History: A Selected Research Bibliography.* Little Rock: Department of Arkansas Natural and Cultural Heritage, 1984.

Hanson, Gerald T., and Carl H. Moneyhon. *Historical Atlas of Arkansas.* Norman: University of Oklahoma Press, 1989.

Lancaster, Bob. *The Jungles of Arkansas: A Personal History of the Wonder State.* Fayetteville: University of Arkansas Press, 1989. There are numerous histories, many more formal and comprehensive or more formal and selective. This particular history provided me the most pleasurable read.

The Made Thing: An Anthology of Contemporary Southern Poetry. Edited by
Leon Stokesbury. Fayetteville: University of Arkansas Press, 1987.

Ozark, Ozark: A Hillside Reader. Edited by Miller Williams. Columbia:
University of Missouri Press, 1981.

Randolph, Vance, and George P. Wilson. *Down in the Holler: A Gallery of
Ozark Folk Speech.* Norman: University of Oklahoma Press; third print-
ing, 1986. Especially useful is the chapter titled "The Dialect in
Fiction."

The Roads of Arkansas. William H. Burdett. Fredericksburg, Tex.: Shearer
Publishing Company, 1990. With special thanks to Bob Lancaster for
his contribution to the lists of cafes, movies, place names, weather facts,
and famous people.

The Scrapbook of Arkansas Literature: An Anthology for the General Reader.
Editor-in-chief, Octavius Coke. Edited by Maj. Troy W. Lewis.
American Caxton Society Press, 1939.

The state of Arkansas is fortunate to have three presses whose lists include
the state and its writers as a cultural treasure: August House Publishers, Inc.,
Rose Publishing Company, and the University of Arkansas Press. Any study has
to begin with the new titles they continue to bring out and the ones they continue to recover from our written record.

C. D. Wright was born in Mountain Home, Arkansas. She moved to Boone County when she was in the first grade for her father to assume the chancery and probate court bench. She graduated from Harrison High School and completed her master's in fine arts at the University of Arkansas. Her brother, a psychologist, lives in Harrison with his wife, Linda, a native of Newton County. Her mother, a retired court reporter, comes from Cotter on the White River. Her mother's family have mostly been railroad people. Her father, the judge, grew up on a small farm near Cisco in Carroll County. Wright has published three chapbooks and four full-length collections of poetry. She has been the recipient of a number of awards and fellowships for writing; the Lila Wallace-Reader's Digest Writer's Award made this project possible. With poet Forrest Gander, Wright edits Lost Roads Publishers, an independent book press founded by the late Frank Stanford of Arkansas. She is on the faculty at Brown University in Providence, Rhode Island.

Deborah Luster is descended from two pioneer Arkansas families. The Pyeatts were among Arkansas Post's first arrivals and later helped settle both Crystal Hill and Cane Hill. The Gunters were one of the founding families of the area once known as The Seven Springs, later Siloam Springs, in Arkansas hill country where Deborah grew up. Currently, she lives in North Carolina, where she is a photographer and codirects the North Carolina Coastal Folklife Project with her husband, Mike Luster.

Also by C. D. Wright

Alla Breve Loving (1976)

Room Rented by a Single Woman (1978)

Terrorism (1979)

Translations of the Gospel back into Tongues (1982)

Further Adventures with You (1986)

String Light (1991)

Just Whistle, with photographs by Deborah Luster (1994)